The Lost Time of TB:
A Daughter's Story

Eileen Sypher

Goose River Press
Waldoboro, Maine

Copyright © 2023 Eileen Sypher

All rights reserved. No part of this book may be reproduced in any form without written permission from the publisher, except by a reviewer who may quote brief passages in a review to be printed in a newspaper or magazine.

Library of Congress Card Number: 2023938983

ISBN: 978-1-59713-261-9

First Printing, 2023

Cover photo by John Yrchik.

Published by
Goose River Press
3400 Friendship Road
Waldoboro ME 04572
e-mail: gooseriverpress@gmail.com
www.gooseriverpress.com

Table of Contents

Prologue//v

Chapter I   New York City 1907–8. A Milk Bottle//1

Chapter II   The Connecticut Cow Barn 1908–1930s//9

Chapter III   First Shadows//25

Chapter IV   Gone Fishin'//36

Chapter V   Speaking Pain//46

Chapter VI   The Red-Brick Sanatorium 1951–2//59

Chapter VII   Going In//75

Chapter VIII   Surgery//96

Chapter IX   The Long After //103

Selected Sources//109

Acknowledgements//113

For my brother
Edward Sypher

Prologue

Our dead continue to live on in us. We remember them. Sometimes we may even speak to them, even though we know they can't speak back. For years, though, I seemed barely even to remember my father. He had become too much like the name we share, a cipher. The photographs of him, of us, were stored away in inaccessible albums. He left me no written words and but a few dim memories. And none who knew him well spoke of him much to me.

At 5 ½, in 1952, I lost my father to the world's still most rampant disease, tuberculosis. A culture of sparing children grief, a mother's need to survive herself, the quiet stigma in a community that shrouded tuberculosis: all had the effect of sealing him up in the grave.

I do not know why I should, seventy years later, have felt a compulsion to resurrect him. Perhaps it was the unrelenting culture of death during the current pandemic, the witnessing of so many children losing parents, the fear that stigma would once again silence talk of how they died. Perhaps it was some altruistic need to show other young people how to remember. Perhaps it was the insistent series of small eruptions

Eileen Sypher

over the years. Perhaps it is my nearing my own end time. Whatever the causes, because of this book he now fills part of the frame of my life as he never did before. And I am grateful. I am completed. A lopped-off limb has grown back. Do I know him now? I do not know. But in my struggling to imagine, to piece-together, the life he lived and the illness that killed him I have come much closer.

I remember, or maybe I imagine, the moment I heard the news. I was in the farmhouse kitchen when the door opened, the handle turned by my uncle. My mother followed him inside. It was a hot day in June. My grandmother, standing by the Dahlstrom table with the red vinyl chairs, had just finished making strawberry shortcake. I remember no words. I only saw her drop the shortcake on the floor. I felt as if I were in a cloud in the ceiling or hiding behind a door.

Then I said nothing even when someone, I think the minister, told me when he took me out for a drive later that afternoon. Six months later I said to my mother, "take me to Daddy's grave." And then I said little about him after that. My mother would often say, "not a day goes by that I don't think of your father." I didn't say anything then either.

Underground rivers have their way. When I was in my 40s and in therapy, two therapists coaxed me while I lay on the floor under blankets, eye shades and headphones on. The therapists made notes of my smallest movements and words. Very quickly I became a small child again, lying in my bed in a room utterly without

The Lost Time of TB: A Daughter's Story

light. There was no one else in the house. Foxes were crying outside my window. As I shuddered, one of the therapists whispered, "do not be afraid, this is a place you already know." I knew then what that dark absence was inside of me. I stayed in that intimately known, so familiar place for a while. But. at the end, I was suddenly sitting in daylight in the open field behind the house. White light exploded within and all around me. A little chink of light had gotten through.

During the summer after, my mother called to tell me that the swamp maple my father had planted by our house had been cracked open by lightning. He had carried the little maple from the edge of that field. It was now fully grown. I wrote my first poem about that tree, about my father's "ancient gesture: planting a shade tree for our new home." We tried to save the tree for years but failed. I wept when it was felled.

Ten years later, seeing a different therapist, I brought in two photographs taken by my mother in different years. I do not know what prompted me to do this. My mother, the photographer, is standing in the same place on the lawn in each. In the earlier one, she has pointed the camera at my father kneeling by our birdbath. He is supporting me, six months old, so I can stand securely to face the camera. Smiling, he looks strong, sinewy, his shirtsleeves rolled up. My face, too, is one large smile. In the other, later photo, I am about eight. She has pointed the camera at me. I stand alone on the sidewalk across the driveway. I am looking at that same birdbath, which now is empty. My posture

Eileen Sypher

is slouched, my mouth drooping. All the early photographs of me are like this, after 1952.

Then there were the accidental moments. I was at a dance outside of Baton Rouge, La. I saw a young father sweep his young daughter off the floor and dance around the room holding her. In another, I was driving by a frozen lake in Connecticut. I saw another young father skating with his young daughter. Agonizing, suddenly piercing these.

After my mother died in 1996, I became curious about my father's family, who had been largely absent from our lives. I began to visit his remaining brothers and sister, who lived not ten miles from me. I began, tentatively, to ask them questions about him (with no response). I grew interested in that family's genealogy so I could make up a past for him, a life lived long before me. He became more solid this way, though more separate. I traced his middle name, Reuben, to his great grandfather, a sawmill keeper, for whom he was clearly named. "Reuben," a name I loved as a child but which perplexed me because I'd never heard it spoken elsewhere. I imagined my father's grandmother Mary meeting her husband Abraham when she went to buy a hat in his shop in Brooklyn. I hunted for photographs. In the earliest one I found of him, he was about ten, bundled up in a winter coat and hat, shoulders slightly hunched, looking somehow overwhelmed. He seemed shy of the camera, uncomfortable. Was he sick then?

And then, over ten years later: the decisive eruption.

The Lost Time of TB: A Daughter's Story

I had taken a young girl shopping in Meriden, Connecticut. She had been my neighbor. One day as we were leaving the mall near where she lived, car window open, she reached her hand out the window and, pointing to a wooded area off to her right, started talking excitedly. "I walked in there once. Awful things went on there. It is abandoned now, but they used to treat the patients horribly, mental patients."

At that moment it happened. I said, "Undercliff." That is "Undercliff." Indeed it was. A place I had forgotten about. Undercliff Sanatorium for Tuberculosis, later mental hospital. I knew the place too well.

My mother would take me there sometimes. It was 1951 and 1952. She could go inside. I could not. I was five, sitting alone on the blanket she had laid down for me on what seemed a vast lawn. I was looking up at small windows in a tall brick building, the highest building I'd ever seen. I was looking up for a face I couldn't see, a face that was looking down on me, a face I would never see again.

Red brick, tall, the sanatorium was intimidating to a small child used to a small house in a field, a house in which I could go in and out of rooms. These walls kept me out. This door was locked to me. I keep trying to find pictures of it as it was then, in 1951. But all I have are earlier photos, when it was made of wood, and then later, interior photos when it briefly housed the elderly. All those beds were lined up in one large room. My father's years are not photographed. For a time the abandoned site became the stuff of ghost hunters.

Eileen Sypher

Abysmal decay. Graffiti on the walls. Chairs with their stuffing torn out. Boxes of records scattered over the floors. Ceilings falling down. Dirt. Decay.

My mother went inside during those days in the early 1950s, but she did not talk about it. In 1994, two years before she died, she wrote me a set of vignettes of her life. She tucked them under the attic eaves—hoping, she wrote, I would find and read them when I too was eighty (I beat her estimate by a few years). My brother, who still lives in our birth house next door to mine, found the box and brought it up to me one afternoon, as if it were a perfectly ordinary thing. There it was, in her lovely handwriting, the stories of her life.

There is just one brief chapter on her life with my father. It was a "good, if short life," she says, and he was "a good man." But there is absolutely no mention of his having had TB when she met or married him. She says only that when they lived in New Mexico before my birth, he was gaining weight. Then nothing, until she speaks of my brother's birth in 1950. She says, "When he was 10 months old [the fall of 1950], his father was in the hospital for 11 weeks, then to Undercliff Sanatorium from end of Jan. 1951 until June 1952. He succumbed on June 28, 1952, following lung surgery on June 9, 1952. So the poor little fellow never even knew his father." (She had scratched out the word "died.") That was all.

This silence was her way of keeping the lid on it all, for herself, for us. For two years after she found him dead in bed, she would go out after work into our coun-

The Lost Time of TB: A Daughter's Story

try yard and cut brush for two hours. Sometimes I could hear her crying in our one bathroom, the same one my father had coughed up his blood in. I was listening. And I was watching her cut brush.

xxx

In my memory of those childhood days, we never named what he died of. His illness was like Henry James' figure in the carpet, a unifying pattern right beneath our feet yet invisible all the same, hidden by the elaborate patterns in the oriental rugs of our days. Most illnesses are hidden in the carpet. It's easier for the survivors. A child whose father died of Covid said, "he died of pneumonia." My mother would say, "he died of an embolism." In reality, he died after radical surgery to remove two lobes of his right lung, cut out because he had tuberculosis: TB: otherwise known as consumption, the wasting disease, because it feeds off the body it inhabits. Sometimes it is known as the "white plague." He died at forty-five of the disease that has been around for millennia and still is, so common now that many people have forgotten it. Half the population of England suffered from it in the nineteenth century. In the first half of the twentieth century tuberculosis killed five million people in the United States. In 1952, the year my father died, it was the greatest killer of those between 15 and 30. Tuberculosis began a steady decline in advanced countries as people began to practice sanitary living conditions, knowing it was communicable, and as surgical and eventually pharmaceutical practices lowered death rates. My father, just too late for the drugs, was part of a shrinking remnant. In the world, however, the situation is still dire. TB, until this year of COVID, was the most infectious disease in the world, killing 1.5 million people in 2020, the first increase in a decade.[i] The medicine to cure it doesn't work for those with multidrug-resistant TB, a growing segment. And inequitable distribution of health care stymies its slowing. The Bacille Calmette-Guerin, or BCG, vaccine, around for about ninety years, has been used to vaccinate uncontaminated infants in countries where TB is rampant, but its efficacy remains controversial. It does not prevent primary infection or the reactivation of latent infections.[ii] A disease intertwined with the very history of humanity,[iii] TB threatens to remain so. Even though its name be not spoken. Even as people now attempt to keep Covid off their loved ones' death certificates. Even though people continue to hide it in the carpet, stuff it in the attic, lock it in boxes.

TB, it turns out, has similarities to Covid. Scientists have just discovered Covid is spread by deep exhalations more so than by coughing.[iv] And, as with COVID, some people can spread the TB bacteria to many people, others to few. And not everyone so infected will be symptomatic. At the beginning of the twentieth century, nearly all people in the United States carried the TB germ, were "latent" as it is called. My mother and I carried my father's germs without manifesting any symptoms. Likely all my father's siblings carried the germ.

The Lost Time of TB: A Daughter's Story

In time to come, likely many who never got Covid will still bear its signature.

Here is the rub: the ones who manifest either of these diseases, better hidden than leprosy or polio, yet still bearing its traces in bloody coughs or incurable pneumonia, will be set apart. Or they will set themselves apart. Sometimes it will be subtle, a failure to kiss someone, standing farther away, a guarded look in the eye, but sometimes there will be shunning. No rooms to rent here. No job for you. No playing with my children. And so on and so on.

Even now, years after TB has been controlled here, I feel its power. Everyone I ask now in my small Connecticut town, the town where my father once lived, seems to know someone who had it, who died from it. But they are largely silent. Their stories are so very brief: "yes, when he came back from the sanatorium, after the procedures, he moaned all night in his bed." When I ask for more, she turns away. "My family believed in taking care of their own. They wouldn't let her go to the doctor because they knew he would have her taken away." No details. The memories seem to spin no narratives. The tongues get stopped. Like mine was. That oral history is all but lost in the never telling.

Or maybe they were all also being stalwart in the face of a disease for which there was then no cure, for which there is still no cure for everyone. Or perhaps people are quiet out of shame, shame their relatives got it, shame they infected others. Perhaps my father's

Eileen Sypher

family, brothers, sister, my mother, were ashamed.[v] Perhaps I was. For years when people would ask me about my father, all I would say was, "he died of TB." Had he lived earlier among the middle and upper classes, he, they, might not have been shamed by it. Tuberculosis was not always stigmatized. Earlier in the nineteenth century, on the contrary, it was often romanticized, seen as a hereditary disease of artists. It became the stuff of opera. Women would paint their faces white; gauntness was the look.[vi] As long as tuberculosis seemed confined to a specific group of people through heredity, the rest of us didn't have to worry. Of course, for those who had it, and for their families, it was ghastly, but hidden away in dim rooms.

It took a long time for people to give up the hereditary notion, long after 1882 when Robert Koch first discovered the microbe responsible for TB.[vii] TB seemed unlike other diseases readily accepted as contagious. It has a latency period when the patient is not symptomatic. "Constant, pervasive, and persistent,"[viii] the distance between exposure and active illness can be very long. Once people slowly accepted the idea of its being contagious, the question became, what conditions facilitated its spread? Repeated close contact abetted by people's living conditions: If one lived in a crowded place without good ventilation, if one hadn't proper nutrition, TB spread more rapidly. "Cure," before antibiotics, meant space, fresh air, nutritious food, rest—all preventives the poor didn't have. Since there was to be no cure for another sixty years or so,

The Lost Time of TB: A Daughter's Story

the afflicted were often stigmatized. "They" didn't live well enough, and "they" were infecting the rest of us. The quotation I abhor on this comes from, of all people, a doctor in Ireland in 1912, a member of the National Association for the Prevention of Tuberculosis. "Tubercule is in truth a coarse common disease, bred in foul breath, in dirt, in squalor...the beautiful and rich receive it from the unbeautiful poor...tubercule attracts failures."[ix] Even now, I come across the refrain, "it is a disease of the poor."

It is time now for me to find the figure in the carpet. To open more boxes in the attic. To imagine, to explore, a silenced, lost history, his history yes, both outside and inside, what I can piece together of it, but also that of a generation, one situated in the rural dairy land of Connecticut in the first half of the twentieth century. A life situated. As Woolf says, "our minds are all threaded together."[x] He will become more real to me then. The story begins in his birthplace in New York City in 1907, where his father had likely already contracted tuberculosis while he was selling the tainted milk of that era. Perhaps my father's nursing mother passed it on to him. Then I go with them to the 100 acre farm in Connecticut to which the family fled in 1908, having been warned of the unhealthiness of the City and having already lost several children. I see inside the English barn, right up the road from me now, where my father spent hours with the cows, cows likely infected with another strain of TB, mycobacterium bovis, but one that spreads to humans. I go inside his life in the

Eileen Sypher

small, rural town he grew in, where others knew you had it. With trepidation, removing my hands from my eyes that for so long blocked out graphic images of TB, I go even inside his body, beginning to be ravaged by the gnawing, slow disease. How could my father, I wonder, imagine he could get married, when women were discouraged from taking tubercular husbands? I travel with both of them to New Mexico, where he hoped to feel better, and did for a time. And then I need to go with them back home, where I then came into the picture, and, then, but three years later, into that red-bricked sanatorium, home for so many, from which I was locked out. I need even, at the last, to go with him to the hospital, where they would remove two lobes of his right lung, "so you could have a life with your children," the doctors told him. There, at last, I will sit with him as he lay dying, days later, alone.

Throughout, my father knew he had a chronic disease, one for which there was no cure. While he could not number his days, he knew, better than many of us, that his days did have a number. I wonder how he lived his days knowing this. A close friend who died four years ago from chronic leukemia complications showed me how. She was still so alive throughout her suffering, dressing with care, going to the opera, baking, doing her needlepoint. And so was he. So I will go there too, go into his great love—fishing.

I try to be fair to him, though I know, as Woolf also says, one can never "sum up" a life. I know I am a filter. My own hunger animates me. My education intrudes.

The Lost Time of TB: A Daughter's Story

And my language, he who never went past the 9th grade. I am sometimes piecing the quilt of his life. I may not get it all quite right. And my story of his illness, my pathography, is out of step with his time, neither his class or his wider culture welcoming pain narratives, as our own does. My father, rather, grew in the stalwart time, the time when people grinned and bore it. And he was also humble. I hope he doesn't mind my trying to open his mouth.

---

[i] Report from the World Health Organization, *New York Times*, October 14, 2021

[ii] Ibid. See also Medica, *The Journal of Clinical Medicine*, (March 2013, 891), pp. 53–58.

[iii] Thomas Goetz, *The Remedy*, Gotham (New York, 2014), 90.

[iv] *New York Times*, October 19, 2021.

[v] *The Remedy* links TB's stigma, along with those of other diseases, to the misapplication of Darwin: if one were ill, one was being culled from the fittest. 100.

[vi] Katherine Byrne. *Tuberculosis and the Victorian Literary Imagination.* Cambridge Univ. Press (Cambridge, 2011).

[vii] Had my father lived earlier among some New England farmers, who saw that whole families were often afflicted, he might have had this family history. Some families dug up a recently interred tubercular relative. If they found blood still in the heart, they took this to mean the dead one was drawing the life from the living. Their solution was to cut out a brother's, a sister's, a parent's heart and burn it. See Michael Bell, *Food for the Dead: On the Trail of New England's Vampires*, Garnet Press, 2011.

[viii] *The Remedy*, 90.

Eileen Sypher

[ix] Dr. Woodcock from the National Association for the Prevention of Tuberculosis, speaking in 1912. Quoted in Susan Kelly, "Stigma and Silence: Oral Histories of Tuberculosis," Oral History, Vol 39, no. 1, Discrimination, Spring 2011, 65.

[x] The Diaries of Virginia Woolf, 1 July 1903.

Chapter I

New York City 1907-1908. A Milk bottle

My father's story begins thirty-nine years before I was born—in New York City. For me his origin story is anchored in the milk bottle that now sits in my window. A young man, who had recently lived in the Connecticut farmhouse my grandparents moved to in 1908 when they left the City, found the bottle in the corner of the barn. One day he approached me in church and asked if I would like it. Cracked on the rim, it bears the name, "Oakwood Farm, F. J. Sypher." F. J.: Frank Joseph, my grandfather. As the Celts say, holding the object of one's ancestor releases the spirit. Maybe that is the day my voyage into my father's family and my father began. For my father's early life was all about milk, unpasteurized milk, milk that my mother never let me drink. Did she know? Was milk what killed him?

My father's life began in an apartment in New York City in January 1907, among the first glass milk bottles. His father Frank made his living in the city by selling milk in these bottles, as he later proudly advertised when he sold his own milk in Connecticut a few years later. Frank was born in Mt. Kisco, Westchester,

1

Eileen Sypher

New York in 1872 into a German-Dutch family of farmers and sawmill keepers. He moved to New York City sometime before his marriage in 1894 to Cornelia Brower, daughter of a prosperous Dutch Brooklyn hatter. The newly married couple lived with Cornelia's widowed father, Abraham or Abram, a couple of boarders, a servant, and another Brower relative and his wife on the then upper west side of 5th avenue, on 57th Street. The Browers had regularly moved north in the city as their family grew and as TB contagion on the Lower East Side, in the so-called "lung blocks," spread.

Sifting through photographs left by cousins at the local historical society (we did not have them), I found none of that apartment, nor baby pictures of my father. But I found evidence of a whole new family. Cornelia, for example, my grandmother whom I never knew but was named partly after. Her baby pictures, indicative of her prosperity, suggest her later stoutness. I found I looked a little like her. The trove opened a bloodline and a history.

During the twelve years Frank and Cornelia lived in New York City they had seven children, of whom only four survived. The last of them was my father. The only photograph I have of my father's first home was taken outside outside before he was born. His great grandfather Reuben and his daughter, Rafelia, had come from Mt. Kisco, likely to visit Reuben's grandson Frank's first child, also Frank, then a baby. Reuben is sitting outside on a bench, Rafelia by his side. In the background stands a four-story apartment building.

The Lost Time of TB: A Daughter's Story

Billowing white sheets hang out of every window. Reuben died before my father Edward was born, never knowing the grandson who would bear his middle name.

The pictures don't tell the whole story of my father's infancy. For that I have to turn to social history to try to understand why three babies died and why my grandfather Frank may already have contracted the disease that would kill him ten years later and show up in my father when they lived in Connecticut. Frank's own father had died young, of sepsis, which can be caused by untreated tuberculosis. Perhaps Frank carried the microbe in a latent form, only to have it blossom in the infected city, a microbe he may have passed on to my infant father. Whatever, New York City then was a fertile ground for the incubation and transmission of tuberculosis. New York had just over one million inhabitants when Frank went there to begin working. By the time he and Cornelia left, there were nearly five million. The influx of immigrants strained the city's infrastructure. Crowding in unsanitary conditions in Lower East Side tenements was legion. And with the crowding blossomed infectious diseases, among them, tuberculosis. By 1900, tuberculosis was the leading cause of death in the United States, causing about one out of every nine deaths, with ten percent of them or more having contracted the bovine form of the disease.[i]

For more reasons than overcrowding and poor sanitation, New York City was particularly susceptible to incubating and transmitting tuberculosis. In 1911 the

Eileen Sypher

Director of the Bureau of Municipal Research in Philadelphia, Jesse Burks, Ph.D., began his report, "Clean Milk and Public Health," with the statement, "Behind its veil of opaque whiteness, every quart of milk hides a potential peril to the public health." Milk, he says, can be the carrier of epidemics such as "typhoid, scarlet fever, diphtheria and septic sore throat."[ii] And, it carried tuberculosis.[iii] The unpasteurized milk my grandfather sold was dangerous.

In turn-of-the-century New York City, milk was a major problem. The demand for it grew exponentially, while there was less and less room for dairy cows to be stabled in the city. Feeding the cows sheltered there was difficult so they were often fed the grain mash from the whiskey distilleries. This made the cows sick. They could barely stand up and lived in filthy conditions indoors. They produced thin blue milk called "swill milk." As many as half of the children under five were dying of the diseases this milk carried—tuberculosis, typhoid, diarrhea.[iv] By the late 1840s the pure milk movement was launched and by 1875 a law was passed prohibiting the sale of swill milk. But in 1904 thousands of cows were still fed slop in Brooklyn.[v]

The milk delivered from outside the city was also often tainted. Unrefrigerated, unpasteurized, milk took 24 to 48 hours after being drawn from the cows to be delivered to the city. Though Burks maintains that the milk would have "kept," it was still often adulterated, preserved with toxic compounds and teeming with bacteria. In the 1880s "an analysis of milk in New Jersey

The Lost Time of TB: A Daughter's Story

found the 'liquifying colonies [of bacteria] to be so numerous that the researchers simply abandoned the count."[vi] Milk was thinned, then recolored with plaster dust or pureed calf brains to make it look creamy. And, if the milk were near to souring, the dairymen would add formaldehyde to stop it from decomposing. This was the dairymen's solution to concerns about tainted milk carrying pathogens. Rivaling Upton Sinclair's later expose in 1906 of the pork-producing industry in *The Jungle*, Hurty, from the Indiana health department, catalogued in late 1800 the worms, hair, insects, blood, pus and manure often found in milk. His response to the argument that formaldehyde killed pathogens? "'Well, it's embalming fluid that you are adding to milk. I guess it's all right if you want to embalm the baby.'" It wasn't until 1905 that New York City mandated the licensing of milk traders. In 1906, a year before my father was born, federal regulations were put in place to prevent these practices.[vii]

Aside from how local cows were fed or what was added to whatever milk there was loomed an even larger problem: some milk was coming from tubercular cows and no one could tell which were healthy. There was neither infrastructure for accounting for the source of the milk nor uniform testing of the cows for *mycobacterium bovis*, the tubercular microbe cows carried. The rural districts which supplied milk to New York City were as much as 350 miles away.[viii]

When the public realized that diseased cows could cause tuberculosis in humans (something Koch himself

Eileen Sypher

discounted at first), they wanted to eradicate the cows rather than pasteurize their milk. People shrank from drinking milk from cows that were diseased, even though pasteurization would have killed the bacteria. But the mapping and eradication of diseased cows at these distances, a mapping contested by rural areas not wanting big city interference, was a nightmare. In addition, myths about pasteurization flourished. People claimed it changed the taste of the milk. It made the milk more expensive. Even some physicians argued that a small amount of *mycobacterium bovis* in the milk could help children develop resistance to TB. Others argued that farmers would become lax in the care of their cows if pasteurization were mandated.[ix] Then there was the issue of cost to the farmers of pasteurizing, many of whom did not have electricity. Pasteurization would not become standard practice until the 1930s, a long way from 1899 when a Harvard microbiologist, Theobald Smith, argued that pasteurization could kill this pathogen. Milk pasteurization in New York did not begin until 1912, though mandated in 1910, leading a decade later to a 50% reduction in non-pulmonary TB deaths (which is where bovine TB contracted through milk usually manifests).[x]

My grandfather Frank, whatever he didn't know about the milk he was selling, certainly knew the difference between formaldehyde-colored milk and cream. My grandmother, Cornelia, mother of four by 1908, likely nursing, was surely nervous. I have one of her household journals from before her marriage. She

The Lost Time of TB: A Daughter's Story

clearly was very conscious of all the items brought into the house. She likely owned a copy of Fannie Farmer's cookbooks, one of which was *Food and Cookery for the Sick and Convalescent*, published in 1903. In it Farmer warns homemakers of the " 'unappetizing and unhealthful pollution' of commercially sold [unpasteurized] milk."[xi] Cornelia was also likely roused into action by magazines such as What to Eat (which featured an article entitled "How to Detect Food Adulterations"), Bulletin 100, designed for the public by the USDA, *Some Forms of Food Adulteration and Simple Methods for their Detection*, and a three-part series on food adulteration published in the popular *Woman's Home Companion* in 1905.[xii] Homemakers were increasingly being urged to look closely at the products they fed their children.[xiii]

Things in the family came to a head. Living in the city was dangerous to one's health. Frank would soon stop selling milk on the streets and become an electrician, a lineman, for a short while. Soon they would flee the city entirely.

---

[i] Alan L. Olmstead and Paul W. Rhode, "An Impossible Undertaking: The Eradication of Bovine Tuberculosis in the United States," *The Journal of Economic History*, vol. 64, no. 3 (September 2004), 734–5.

[ii] "The Annals of the American Academy of Political and Social Science," Vol 37, No 2 *The Public Health Movement*, Sage, March 1911, 196.

[iii] Suzanne Spellen, "Walkabout, The Great Milk Wars," Pt. 1, *The Brownstoner*, Nov. 8, 2011.

Eileen Sypher

[iv] Ibid.

[v] Ibid.

[vi] Deborah Blum, "The 19th-Century Fight Against Bacterial-Ridden Milk Preserved With Embalming Fluid," *The Smihsonian Magazine*, August 22, 2020, previously unpublished excerpt from *Undark*, an online magazine, October 5, 2018, 1–4.

[vii] Blum.

[viii] Susan D. Jones, "Mapping a Zoonotic Disease: Anglo-American Efforts to Control Bovine Tuberculosis Before World War I," Osiris, 2004, 2nd Series, Vol 19, 139.

[ix] Ibid., 144-5.

[x] Margaret Good, et. al., "The History of In Vivo Tuberculin Testing in Bovines: Tuberculosis, a 'One Health' Issue," Frontiers in Veterinary Science, April 9, 2019.

[xi] Deborah Blum, *The Poison Squad*, Penguin (New York, 2018), 99.

[xii] Ibid., 126.

[xiii] Ibid., 110–11.

Chapter II

The Connecticut Cow Barn 1908-1930s

In 1908, the family got out of New York City, taking Cornelia's, my grandmother's, urbane hatter father and their four remaining children with them, including my infant father. As my mother told it, my grandfather's doctor recommended Frank move out of the city into the country for his health. Like so many others in Manhattan, they had moved north to escape the "lunger blocks" in the city's southern end. But why such a big move? I hunt for a motive. Did he already show signs of the TB that would kill him eighteen years later? If so, did he fear the stigma of TB that he observed while living in the city—because he sold possibly tainted milk? Or did the three children they lose while they lived there die from TB?

And which TB did he or his children possibly carry? Sometime before his death in Conn. in 1926, Frank, whenever he contracted the disease initially, developed active tuberculosis. Was it the more typical strain, *mycobacterium tuberculosis*, or the bovine strain, *mycobacterium bovis*, both of which can infect humans? If the second strain, was this because he sold milk (the symptoms are the same)? The bovine

Eileen Sypher

form was more prevalent in the cities, where the cows were crowded into small spaces, as were people, although farmers in rural areas were also infected by their cows. His death certificate says only "Pulmonary Tuberculosis, secondary cause Tubercular Meningitis." Meningitis: an unimaginable way to die in 1926.

People did not know at the turn of the last century that cows carrying TB could infect them. The spaciousness of the country, replete with cows, seemed to offer some promise of safety from the increasingly crowded conditions that seemed to spread disease. Many physicians urged their ill patients to seek rural climates with fresher air. Although Robert Koch in 1882 had learned that tuberculosis was not hereditary nor curable by fresh air alone, but rather spread by the infectious microbe he had discovered, it took a while for people, including doctors, to absorb the implications of this. In the absence of any biological cure, people relied on the earlier solutions: get to a healthier climate, spread out, practice better living conditions. Drier climates were seen as preferable for those suffering from tuberculosis. Susan Sontag says, "'There was a notion...that tuberculosis was a wet disease, a disease of humid and dank cities. The inside of the body became damp and had to be dried out.' "[i]

My grandparents bought a hundred ten acres in the woods, a farmhouse and a barn to the far east of the city in a small Connecticut town, Chester. I wonder if local people looked kindly on their arrival. A neighbor of mine in Chester, where I too live again, said that his

The Lost Time of TB: A Daughter's Story

mother always blamed the influx of TB in the town on people who had visited relatives in New York and returned.[ii]

When Frank moved to the country, there were 22,000 farms in Connecticut, 4,900 of them a hundred acres, the size of his. In 1910, over twenty thousand of them were devoted to milk production. My father grew up during the years when the small family dairy farm was still a viable way of making a living. My father, the youngest when they arrived, likely first started to walk in cow pastures. I am sure my grandparents hoped their cows were clean. I am sure they hoped that they had left the milk wars behind them. I am sure they hoped their children would be safe. This was not to be.

At this point in my pieced-together story, I have many more photos to help me. In one, two women are wearing long skirts. I recognize the barn they are standing in front of. It is the red cow barn still standing up the road. This photo must have been taken before the Great War, just after they moved from the city. A pair of sturdy oxen yoked in the fore front, a young man in knickers and a young girl stand between them and the two women. A man stands behind them. Their oldest son, their only girl, their mother (my grandmother, Cornelia), my grandmother's Aunt Mary, and my grandfather Frank. My father was but crawling nearby when this picture was taken around 1908. He may have been looking up at them. The animals are front and center. Cow pride. A new life.

I have another, slightly later photo of an older man

Eileen Sypher

wearing a three-pieced suit and a hat, leaning against a fence in a meadow, four children near him. I peer and peer at them but can't quite tell if one is my three-year old father. The man was my great grandfather Abraham, widower, the hatter, who moved with them to the farm from New York at 75 to help raise a new generation. He looks dapper, out of place in a field, rather unsuited for farming. He brought with him to Connecticut tintypes and ambrotypes, expensive photographs, of his sister Mary and his brother Alexander Ramsay, and perhaps one of his own wife Mary, Cornelia's mother, who had died at 51, seventeen years after giving birth to her only child. All are wearing expensive clothing. He would have wanted to look at them by his bed every morning and evening to remind himself of those he left behind, and perhaps of his abandoned urban life as well. He also brought with him a small leather-bound book of William Blake's *Songs of Innocence*, the discovery of which reminds me I somehow fit into this family. Abraham was a book binder. Perhaps he had bound this very 1850 version. When he died in 1910, two years after coming to the Connecticut Farm, he wanted his body shipped back to his beloved New York for burial.

My grandfather Frank dug even deeper into his farming roots when he moved to Connecticut in 1908 to start the dairy farm. The house and English-style barn were already built. Willoughby Lynde, whose family owned--and still own--a lot of land around the old homestead, was a member of one of the first families to

The Lost Time of TB: A Daughter's Story

come from England. Willoughby bought the land and built the house and English-style barn in 1835. This was not a place where people moved around a lot.

I suspect the money to purchase the farm came from my grandmother's family. Though she likely didn't sign on to be a farmer's wife, moving was a way to save her husband's likely weak health and certainly her infant children. I don't know if Cornelia ever warmed to farm life. Her family were urban. But there she was with a farmer husband and four living children. In the prolific way of the Dutch in those years, three more children were to come.

All of them lived together in a farmhouse that still stands, although it has been renovated. With seven children and four bedrooms upstairs, there was little space separating people when they were inside. But that was very typical of New England farmhouses. Despite what we would call overcrowding, there was ventilation aplenty—the old farmhouse was poorly insulated. Even with two people in the house suffering from tuberculosis at different times, and likely more carrying the latent germ, the farmhouse was not nearly as toxic as New York's tenements. All the same, it was impossible to live isolated when one was sick.

Frank must have learned a lot from his family in Westchester, New York about dairy farming, for it is not an easy job for a novice. All my father would tell my mother about his childhood was that the work was hard. John Connell's recent book, *The Farmer's Son: Calving Season on a Family Farm*, gives me a glimpse

Eileen Sypher

into my father's work.[iii] A son, an aspiring writer, has come back to work the farm with his difficult father. Connell's narrative of dairy farming shows how exhausting yet exhilarating the work is. Early hours, late nights, midnight awakenings, waiting for and then helping calves to be born. Digging graves for the calves who didn't make it. Cleaning out the stalls and laying fresh hay which the cows liked. Pitching the hay into the barns. Performing rudimentary veterinary work on them. Taking them to market. Grieving their death and managing their selling. Shying away from naming them, yet there were names still, "the red cow." Spending hours and hours alone with them, recognizing how not to disturb a sleeping cow, learning how to calm it, scratching her back to soothe her, wishing, Connell says, one could fully communicate with them.

Farming, according to Connell, is also the most dangerous job. Even if one didn't have expensive machinery, which my family didn't, the cow could kick, the manure was slippery, the bull hard to manage (for my grandparents had a bull—no artificial insemination yet). It was dangerous and tense work. Connell and his father are often at it, his father blaming the son for inattention. I wonder if this was part of my father's difficult history with his father, for he would say nothing else about him.

The milking itself, the hardest task of all the jobs, was likely done by hand since the farm was too small for the milking machines (the older ones didn't require electricity). The average size of dairy farms at that time

The Lost Time of TB: A Daughter's Story

was 5–20 head. There was no refrigeration then (electricity was not common until 1930 or so), so no pasteurization. The milk had to be delivered immediately. The remainder was kept in a lovely little building filled with ice that my mother called "The Creamery." I loved the sound of that word when I was a child and I loved the look of it, a small stone building. My mother would often take me in a carriage from our house nearby up the hill to the old farmhouse to look at it, always speaking, with reverence, the words, "The Creamery." I don't believe they ever made cheese, only butter, as a way of preserving the milk. And I don't know to whom they delivered the milk. There were several other dairy farms in Chester at the time, so they must have stuck close to home. There was likely a cheese-making farm somewhere close by—so one of the deliveries could have been to that.

Frank would have read the bi-annual pamphlets published by what became the Connecticut Milk Regulation Board in 1917. The Connecticut Board of Health Bulletins gave the monthly statistics for diseases by town (TB ranked just behind pneumonia in 1914–15). The pamphlets laid out the rules for dairies: inspectors can show up, unannounced, any time; no bottles or cans can be used for anything poisonous (no reference to sanitation); the cream cannot be skimmed unless the customer is told; absolutely no additives were to be added to the milk (clearly the stories of the city's tainted milk made it to Connecticut)—in fact the subject of adulteration occupies many of the prohibi-

Eileen Sypher

tions for Connecticut food sales. These pamphlets are revealing for what is left out: recommended pasteurization isn't mentioned until after 1915. Tuberculosis from milk as a problem isn't mentioned at all in 1906. Then the additions: in 1914–15, persons who have a disease should stay away from cows and milking; in 1923 the sale of milk from diseased cows is prohibited. No person with TB should handle milk containers, etc. TB shows up rather late in the public literature of regulation.[iv]

Farming indeed was intense business. And it was a potentially lethal business. The hands that milked and the hands that calved were intimate with the animals. If just one cow were sick (and if the barn wasn't ventilated well), disease could spread. But no one could tell in the early stages whether a cow were sick, for cows were usually asymptomatic—though still contagious.[v] Droplets of saliva from a cow's cough could infect a human as would her unpasteurized milk. In 1900 fifteen percent of TB deaths were caused by the bovine form and by 1915 ten percent of the cows in the United States were infected with this germ.[vi]

Frank died in 1926 when my father was 18. He made his will out in March and was dead by September, leaving the land, worth $3490, five cows, a pair of oxen, a horse, two pigs, a Graham tractor, and two overland trucks. And he left the family in debt by $1000, ostensibly from farm-procured debts—although my grandfather was apparently also a gambler. In one photograph all the children, except my father, who took

The Lost Time of TB: A Daughter's Story

the photo as he often did (isolation?), are standing spread out in front of the farmhouse, their father off to the side. No one seems close to anyone else. Perhaps it was really like that. Perhaps they didn't miss him when he died. My mother knew nothing about Frank, nor did any of the other relatives speak of him to my mother. But also, most of my father's siblings didn't send my parents wedding wishes or gifts and most never visited my mother after my father died. Perhaps they were ashamed that Frank and later his son died from TB. Silence was better.

There were in all six boys and one girl. The eldest son married early and ran another dairy farm nearby, and the girl married a local farmer. For a family photo in 1924, however, all the children are proudly lined up in front of the automobiles that were used to deliver the milk. The farm must have started to close down around the time of my grandfather's death in 1926. Before that time, likely the youngest boy, only 12 then, wasn't much help. But there were enough strong boys early on to help my grandfather.

My father may already have had TB by then, passed to him from the cows. My father loved to get close to animals. He spent hours out back in the woods of the house I grew in, the woods I now live in perhaps to get closer to him. My mother would tell stories of how he would try to befriend chipmunks (one bit him). He got so close to a skunk once that it sprayed his leather jacket. He had to bury it. My mother described him as a "compassionate" man. I see him stroking the cow's face, talking to it. And especially if he found his father difficult, these relationships with the animals, time alone in the barn, were what would comfort him.

Mycobacterium bovis, the strain of tuberculosis that is two and a half times more deadly for humans,[vii] was not isolated in cattle until 1882. But even by 1901 Koch continued to claim that tubercular cattle posed no threat to humans, even though veterinarians had become infected and died from it in 1900. Those who campaigned against the disease tried to map the location of infected cows. This proved to be an easier job than enforcing compulsory methods to eradicate the infected animals or, later, to enforce pasteurization once it became available.

The first testing of cows did not happen until 1905, in Michigan, with regular and required testing beginning in Connecticut in 1928, two years after Frank died.[viii] There was a federal mandate in 1917 that all cows in the country be tested, yet it took years for such testing to be universal. By 1940, 3.8 million cows had been destroyed.[ix] The dairy industry and its farmers resisted expensive testing, even as they resisted pasteurization, for which they had to pay. In 1931 in Iowa there were riots, with farmers lining up to attempt to prevent vets from testing their cows. They argued that the test was invalid, that the costs were too high, and that due process was being denied farmers.[x]

Infection in the East remained high. It had taken until 1911 for the state to recognize that the tuberculin test was the only way to ascertain whether a cow was

The Lost Time of TB: A Daughter's Story

ill, but it was not until 1916 that an active eradication program was initiated. At this point 30% of the state's cattle were thought to be infected. It was not until 1919 that the state joined with the Federal Government in the eradication program. When they were done, 77,485 cattle were destroyed. New Hampshire, New York and Vermont had similar projects, also with early opposition.[xi]

Connecticut's largest newspaper, *The Hartford Courant*, offers a window into local sentiment. In 1895 it reported that a hearing on bovine tuberculosis would be held in the legislative chambers. They comment, "it is interesting, not to say surprising, how great a feeling has developed in the matter." The article goes on to mention the position of two opposing sides, with the pro side arguing that cattle can transmit TB to humans and that the available test is accurate, and the con side arguing that interchange between animal and human does not occur and that the test is invalid.

Cows were, however, destroyed. The response of cattlemen to the required slaughter of cows was vigorous. In a case in West Hartford in 1920, reported on at length in *The Courant* on January 28, 1920, 50 of a herd of 59 were slaughtered by order of the Commissioner. Fellow farmers called the Commissioner a "despot" and asked what right he had to do so. They said "he should know better than to order such a wholesale slaughter of cows." The Commissioner is calm, says he is doing his job, and when asked if these cows were tubercular and a menace to the public, replies "they certainly were." He asserts that investigators found a large number of young children afflicted with TB of the bovine type caused by a sick cow's milk. The protestors complain that in the past they have had Commissioners who treated the farmers fairly. They say there is a "war" on cattle and farmers. They want the law changed. The article mentions that farmers were now nervous about these inspections. The piece goes into great depth, describing the horrible sight of the slaughtered cows, the anguish families faced when their herd is destroyed. It then relays a story of a case where a Mr. Granger of Enfield, on being told that a few cows he had just purchased from Buffalo were tubercular, shipped them back to Buffalo only to have a vet pronounce them clean.

Pasteurization, of course, helps save the milk and the cows, although it is not foolproof.[xii] But even when electricity was ample, some dairy men protested pasteurization. One letter to *The Courant's* editor in 1923 chastises the wealthy farmers from West Harford who protest that there are more vitamins in raw milk from a tuberculin-tested cow than from pasteurized milk. This is an argument that continues.[xiii] It would not be until 1936 that the state would declare a successful conclusion to bovine TB eradication.[xiv] Bovine TB was "practically eliminated" in one of the worst infected states in the country.

My grandfather died during the height of the eradication program. I have no information on whether the commission found his cows infected; individual farms

The Lost Time of TB: A Daughter's Story

were not listed in inspection reports. But it is hard to imagine my grandfather not being fully aware of this brewing fear and anger on the part of the state's dairy farmers. He could read. He likely saw the newspapers. He talked with other farmers. It is also hard to imagine him not being depressed. He had left New York after unwittingly selling tainted milk, probably already sick with TB himself, only to start a farm with potentially tubercular cows. Down the road three neighbors in one house had already died, perhaps drinking his milk. And while all this was happening, he was observing his third son, my father, likely falling ill to the same disease that was felling him.

Did my father acquire his TB from the cows? Ten percent of the nation's cows were infected with it, and 20–30% of the people who died from TB carried it.[xv] I will never know which microbe he carried or exactly when my father's TB, likely latent, became activated and by what. This is as far as I can go.

While the cow wars were accelerating in Connecticut, my father and his siblings were growing up. Other than working on the farm, my father, like his brothers, but not his only sister, attended school through the 8th grade. Up until at least 1923, only 6th grade attendance was mandatory, and then for boys only.[xvi] The one-room schoolhouse a half mile from the farm, one of four in the town, had closed down in 1905. After that date, all the children from the town attended a single school. Graduating from the 8th grade and not continuing was, at least in 1918, not considered poor

21

performance. One article in *The Hartford Courant* commends the 8th grade graduates, saying that "many are at the top of the ladder as far as their lives are concerned."[xvii] Clearly, advanced education was not common. Though the certification of elementary teachers at the time mandated completion of high school, this certification was sometimes relaxed depending on the market.[xviii]

I attended grammar school in the same building as my father, perhaps sitting in the same classrooms. I wonder if he had etched his initials under one of the wooden desks, though I don't remember ever looking. When I was in the 6th grade, my class was the last to graduate from the building. It was by then derelict. I remember the basement, dank, dark, the bathrooms where little girls shared secrets and the dark corners where girls hit each other and pulled each other's hair. Like my father, we had recess though, mornings of kick ball, time on the swings, time to share stories and love notes with each other. He likely did the same.

I started going to that school the fall after he died. I had a lot of dreams in those months, often of him, often nightmares. Once I dreamed that a fire destroyed the school. His dog, my dog, Princey, was standing outside. He had been cut in half. I was holding him. My life had been cut in half too. After this, I stopped dreaming of him.

---

[i]Nancy Owen Lewis, *Chasing the Cure in New Mexico*, Museum of New Mexico Press (Santa Fe, 2016), p. 8.

The Lost Time of TB: A Daughter's Story

[ii]I am grateful to Peter Zanardi of Chester, Conn. for sharing his many memories and for his help with local research.

[iii]I have found few descriptions of farm life in this country at this time that register the emotions of farming as fully as Connell's book about Ireland does (John Connell, *The Farmer's Son: Calving Season on a Family Farm*, Houghton, Mifflin, Harcourt (Boston, 2018.) Quentin F. Veit's recent book, *The Bumpy Road: Farm Life in the Great Depression* (ed. Ellen M. Meyer, Willow Bend Press, 2020) provides brief sketches of tools, home life, and animal husbandry in Missouri.

[iv]I am grateful to the Connecticut State Library for making available this material.

[v]Olmstead and Rhodes, 741 and 737.

[vi]Ibid., 739.

[vii]An article by Shaukat, Bilal, et.al., "Human bovine tuberculosis—remains in the differential," *Journal of Medical Microbiology*, Vol. 59, Issue 11, 1 November 2010, claims that bovine tuberculosis has not been completely eradicated, particularly in Europe. Cattle are not the only carriers—and humans can transmit the virus back to animals via breathing. While infection from a cow's milk results in non-pulmonary TB, aerosol infection results in pulmonary TB. This article that says that recent data from San Diego (Rodwell et al., "Tuberculosis from Mycobacterium bovis in binational communities, United States. *Emerg Infect Dis* 2008, 14: 909–916) shows that people infected with m. bovis were more than 2.55 times more likely to die than those infected with *m. tuberculosis*.

[viii]*Hartford Courant*, 10/7/1927.

[ix]Mitchell V. Palmer and W. Ray Waters, "Bovine Tuberculosis and the Establishment of an Eradication Program in the United States: Role of Veterinarians," *Veterinary Medicine International*, 17 May 2011. Online publication.

[x]Alan Olmstead and Paul W. Rhodes, "Not on My Farm! Resistance to Bovine Tuberculosis Eradication in the U.S.," *Journal of Economic History*, Vol 67, No. 3 (Sept 2007). 777.

[xi]*Hartford Courant*, 5/26/1936.

Eileen Sypher

[xii]"Human Bovine Tuberculosis," *Journal of Medical Microbiology*, 59.

[xiii]The argument for raw milk continues. A 2012 article in *The New Yorker* reports on The Rawsome Three, a California group which argued that raw milk is the new pot, only more difficult to get. Arrested not because the milk was raw (raw milk is legal in California) but for other practices, the group and its pro-raw milk, get-back-to-the- old-farms ideology, were supported by none other than Rand Paul, The Tea Party and the Proud Boys. Supporters of raw milk argued that pasteurization destroys good enzymes that protect the immune system and destroys the sweet taste of milk. Dana Goodyear, "Raw Deal," April 30, 2012.

[xiv]*Hartford Courant*, 5/3/1936.

[xv]Olmstead and Rhodes, 2004.

[xvi]*Hartford Courant*, 3/17/1923.

[xvii]*Hartford Courant*, 6/26/1918.

[xviii]*Hartford Courant*, 6/9/1922.

Chapter III

First Shadows

My father, along with two of his brothers, stayed on in the old farmhouse with his mother, while his other siblings went off to marry and settle nearby. The dairy farm had been shut down sometime after my grandfather's death, as many had been during the Great Depression. Perhaps the cows were all discovered as carriers of tuberculosis. My father went to work in a local factory that made metal files. He was what was called a "finisher." The factory's red brick building, in a hollow near a stream below the church I grew in, still stands, now a private home.

On December 4th of 1943, according to a shop notebook in the local historical society, the Tuberculosis Commission of Connecticut sent an x-ray van to another local factory to x-ray twenty workers.[i] Likely the van had come before and stopped at all the nearby factories, including my father's. The State Tuberculosis Commission X-Ray vans were not an unusual sight and were to become more numerous in the years to come, going to schools as well as workplaces.[ii] By 1951, there were community-wide chest x-rays.[iii] What dread people must have felt when seeing the approach of those trucks. They could change one's life. My father lost his job. And he was prevented from serving in WWII, unlike his brothers. No proud pictures of him in uniform graced the mantel.[iv] No flag stands over his grave.

I don't know the exact day in 1943 when my father was x-rayed by the vans. Perhaps he knew before 1943 that he carried active TB. Perhaps he, like Keats, woke one morning to find the tell-tale blood on his pillow.[v] He would know what that was, from his father. But in 1943, likely after that x-ray truck showed up at his workplace, he went to his local doctor who then sent him to the nearby sanatorium for further x-rays. His life working beside others was over.

Doctors were technically required to report all active cases of TB, but reporting was sketchy. Not all doctors reported suspected cases, distrusting the states' ability to help their patients.[vi] Some patients with symptoms lied or never went to the doctor in the first place, not wanting to be shipped off to a sanatorium.[vii] In 1910, for example, the local newspaper spoke of a death from tuberculosis, mentioning that the doctor reported it only two weeks earlier. Another woman died at home in 1911. Yet, however incomplete physician reporting, the surveillance of disease in the United States began with tuberculosis. With the understanding that tuberculosis was spread by a contagious germ, America moved into a period with an "unprecedented degree of regulation."[viii] At war were the doctors protecting the privacy of their patients and the health officials protecting the public.[ix] My father's doctor, later my doctor,

The Lost Time of TB: A Daughter's Story

reported his case. He sent him off to get further x-rays at a local sanatorium, Uncas-on-Thames.[x]

I imagine my father's trip to Uncas in 1943 gave him his first glimpse into his own lungs, perhaps his first glimpse of an x-ray. As now, the doctor has to point to the offending area because the patient doesn't know what he or she is seeing. But that first glimpse of one's skeleton: how unnerving. Thomas Mann says of his character Hans Castorp when he first looks at his own chest x-ray: he "saw exactly what he should have expected to see, but which no man was ever intended to see and which he himself had never presumed he would be able to see: he saw his own grave."[xi]

Did my father tell anyone about those findings in 1943, whose exact date I do not know? His mother would die that June of bladder cancer. She had likely been ill for a while, so perhaps he did not want to confide in her, had he known before then.

Silence was likely preferable for many reasons. I have not been able to find out much about the subtle and not so subtle ways disease stigma played out in my father's small town.[xii] In what Snowden has called "the era of contagion,"[xiii] the general public, at least in the cities, began to view those with tuberculosis as dangerous. People who went off to sanatoria lied about where they were going. Families became secretive.[xiv] As the war efforts cranked up and fear of contagion in the armed forces intensified, sufferers were also viewed as unpatriotic. Snowden says that people in the city became hysterical about postage stamps, library books, coins, beards, all of which contained sputum. Children were sent home from school, people were denied lodging, insurance, and urged not to marry. In 1914, billboards depicted TB as German soldiers. In 1901 The New York Tribune had warned that things were going too far: "The American people and their officials, animated with zeal not according to knowledge, are in danger of going to senseless and cruel extremes in hunting down consumptives."[xv] I know about contemporary cases of people shamed by carrying multi-drug-resistant TB.[xvi] One woman's mother, in Mongolia, upon hearing of her daughter's pulmonary, treatable diagnosis in 2011, responded to the doctor giving the diagnosis: " 'That is impossible. Nobody in our family circle has ever had that filthy disease.' "[xvii]

But what happened in the early twentieth century in the little towns in New England, the rural towns, where the bonds among people were stronger, where dairy farms carrying the disease were plentiful?[xviii] Was TB seen as a public scourge or an individual failure? Surely my father's loss of his job in 1943 marked him in the public eye. Did his neighbors feel sorry for him and commiserate with him, or did they avoid him, shy away from him, knowing he had TB? Did people stop shaking his hand on the street? Did his brothers and sister stay apart? Did they lie to others about what was wrong with him? Would my father's mother let him kiss her? Did they attempt to sanitize his dishes? And how aware might he have been of all these subtle changes now that his diagnosis was revealed?

The Lost Time of TB: A Daughter's Story

I don't know when my father recognized he had TB,[xix] but his family had watched their father die from it years earlier and must have recognized any early symptoms in my father: chronic fatigue, chest pain, weight loss (though they were all thin), and a persistent cough. What does one do, living in a crowded house with a sibling who has a disease that is communicable? If they knew, wouldn't they keep quiet to avoid public scrutiny and protect the farm's viability as long as it was selling milk? And, wouldn't they try to keep apart from him as much as possible? In all the early photographs of his family that I have, my father is usually taking the picture. Even in one of the few I have of him with his mother and a brother, he is sitting close to his mother, his brother widely separated. My father's mother protected him and he adored her. I am not sure about the other siblings.

I tried once to explore his family's thoughts about him, when I was talking alone with my father's younger brother many years later. He, then an old man, was standing on the ground where we were to build our next house, perhaps in the very place where my father had tried to pet chipmunks. I had asked him to give us advice about where to put our new driveway since he had been a builder of roads and driveways. Then I said to him, "What was my father like?" He hesitated. He looked off into the distance and then down at the ground. A tear slowly dropped from his eye and traveled down his cheek. Then he said, "Well, you know, I never really knew him. There were so many of us. We knew only those close to us in age. Your father," he said, "was closest to two other brothers." That was all he said. My father had been his best man at his wedding.

I have thought a lot about this moment. There was something unsettling about it, as if he didn't want to say much or couldn't, and yet his pausing, the tear, the looking down at the ground, tell me there was much more there.

Perhaps the whole family was naturally taciturn. But I hover on the edges of what I also think is an abysmal family silence, a desire to avoid, perhaps fear, perhaps some shame. I remember only one uncle visiting us when my father lived with us in our own home. In the years after my mother's death when I tried to visit his remaining family, no one talked about him even when I asked. One would think someone would say something, "Oh I remember when your father did... ." They didn't.

And, most importantly, I remember no one talking about his illness. An uncle told his son that my father had "pneumonia." I knew he had died from tuberculosis, but this was a forbidden word. The family dug a grave for it. Again, to protect me? To protect their memories? Family silences.

They were not alone, of course. This was the culture they lived in. Because of my search, a neighbor decided to research her family history. She discovered that her grandparents and a child had died of tuberculosis. They lived down the road from the farmhouse. She was never told, nor was her father. The disease

The Lost Time of TB: A Daughter's Story

was everywhere. And so was the silence around it.

I do not know how my father survived financially after he lost his job and his mother died. She had left him part of the money from the sale of her house, but that was 1945. He had a place to live, the old homestead, until it was sold. It says on his death certificate that he was a painter during those years. That would have kept him outside, apart from others.

While my father was still working at the file factory, he used to pick up an elderly man who lived alone to take him to work. The man, Charles Lampe, viewed my father as his son. One day in 1940, Mr. Lampe handed my father the deed to his house and twenty acres of land. As my mother often told the story, they were standing in the driveway when Mr. Lampe handed my father a quit-claim deed, turning the property over to my father immediately. My father went to the town office and had it changed so Mr. Lampe could live out his life there. After Mr. Lampe died in 1942, my father let various relatives live in the house. Likely they gave him rent money.

My mother met my father as she was walking home from the local fair in 1926. She was 15 and he was 19. Driving his car, he and a friend picked up my mother and her friend. My mother went out with him until 1936 when she started working for an accounting company that traveled around the country. She thought of him often, she told me in her memoir. She said she did not know why they had drifted apart. My father dated another woman. It wasn't until 1943, when my mother

31

returned, that they got back together. As my mother told the story in her memoir, she went to my father's mother's funeral in June of 1943. She had always liked his mother, Cornelia, and she her. Cornelia once told my mother she was heartbroken my father had broken off with her, his first love. That June day, my mother was walking, alone, back to her car from Cornelia's grave, when my father came up beside her and took her by the arm. She said, "I knew then he still cared for me." Now of course I wonder if he knew when he met up with her again that day in 1943 that he had active tuberculosis. And, if so, I wonder if he told her.

They dated again for two years. I do not know if my mother was cautious about kissing him, or he of her. But in the photographs they sit close to each other and are sometimes arm in arm. I grew up wondering why it took them so long to marry after they got back together and why they did not marry in their hometown. I used to think my father was working and saving money. He wasn't. He was trying to get better.

Four months after my mother and father rekindled their relationship in the cemetery where his mother had just been buried, my father was at the Woodmen's Sanatorium in Colorado Springs, Colo. Perhaps that fateful 1943 x-Ray was taken just before he left. I found out about Woodmen by accident, from some old photos a relative dropped off at the historical society. My mother never mentioned this period of his life to me. The photos only say, "Woodmen, Colorado." The nurse standing next to my father in front of one of the individ-

The Lost Time of TB: A Daughter's Story

ual cabins gives it away.

This sanatorium was open and free to members of the Woodmen's fraternal organization. My father must have been a member, though Woodmen's would not confirm this for me. I suspect my father, his mother dead, now reconnected with my mother and decided to do something about his newly discovered active TB, so he went there for a "cure." I do not know how long he stayed.

The place was idyllic, according to "A Neighbor's Story of the Modern Woodmen of America Sanatorium," an essay published in 1934. People lived in individual cabins, dining and bathing in common areas. The sanatorium depended on the outside world only for electricity. Patients were to rest for four hours a day, sitting outside; then there were four periods per day to read or walk or participate in a patient workshop. Patients could stay no longer than fourteen months. They were taught how to live after they left. According to the essay, 67% of the patients were improved upon leaving.[xx]

When my father came back to Connecticut his health must have deteriorated. One day early in 1945 my father came into the bank where my mother worked. He said, abruptly, "I am going west. The climate here is not good for my health. Come with me and we will get married." My mother knew she hadn't a choice if she wanted to stay with him. She went.

Eileen Sypher

[i] M.S. Brooks Company Daybook, Chester, Conn. Historical Society.

[ii] In 1948 New York Public Radio produced and disseminated a fourteen minute program called "The Constant Invader, Industrial Resurveys." The programs features one unionized worker in a factory who doesn't show up the day the TB x-ray van is coming around. Two of his colleagues, who stood near him on the line, contract TB and are sent to a sanatorium. A TB worker goes to find the missing man, who at first refuses to submit to x-rays. But then he relents when he finds out his friends have gotten it, likely from them. His x-rays reveal TB and he rooms with his two friends at the sanatorium, who forgive him. Clearly people knew the import of these vans and clearly some were refusing. In a union shop, according to this program, the worker's job will be ready for him when cured. My father's shop was not unionized.

[iii] The Chester Historical Society has an advertisement for a free chest x-ray clinic in 1955, to be held at the United Church and sponsored by the Chester Tuberculosis Society. All results will be "confidential."

[iv] An article from 10 April 1942 in *The Hartford Courant* warns that the state is facing an increase in tuberculosis. There are again waiting lists at the sanatoria. The articles note the "speed-up in industry, migration of workers and their families, shortage in housing, gaps in educational and recreational programs, and urgent need of following up results of medical examinations of those called for selective service." Of paramount concern are the necessity of insuring that those called up for service are healthy and the necessity of managing a doctor shortage. The article also mentions the need to follow up those, like my father, who were rejected from service and who had lost their jobs.

[v] Rene and Jean Dubos, *The White Plague: Tuberculosis, Man, and Society*, New Brunswick, N.J. (Rutgers University Press, 1952), 15.

[vi] Amy L. Fairchild, et. al, "Opening Battles: Tuberculosis and Foundations of Surveillance," *Searching Eyes: Privacy, The State, and Disease Surveillance in America*, Berkeley (University of California Press, 2007), 33.

[vii] Some doctors, however, resisted reporting mandates. Before antibiotics, some felt the state could not help, and they resisted incursions into their domain. Others continued to believe heredity continued to play a role.

The Lost Time of TB: A Daughter's Story

Some were afraid their practices would be hurt. Ibid.

[viii] Sheila M. Rothman, *Living in the Shadow of Death*, New York (Basic Books, 1994), 180.

[ix] Ibid.

[x] One of the great indignities of this project for me concerns Conn. state law. It prevents me from ever accessing the medical records of my father held at the State Archives. The federal statute of limitation is fifty years. Connecticut has no limit.

[xi] Opening Battles, 260.

[xii] For a broader discussion of stigma see Erving Goffman, *Stigma*, Englewood Cliffs, N.J. (Prentice-Hall, 1963).

[xiii] Frank M. Snowden, "Tuberculosis in the Unromantic Era of Contagion." *Epidemics and Society*. New Haven (Yale University Press, 2019).

[xiv] Rothman, 212. This was true at least through the 1930s.

[xv] Ibid., 300.

[xvi] See *Stigmatized: A Mongolian Girl's Journey from Stigma and Illness to Empowerment* by Handaa Enkh-Amgalan (New Degree Press, 2021).

[xvii] Ibid., 1371.

[xviii] Rothman observes that discrimination in cities was far worse, 213.

[xix] Kelly says TB is a "concealable stigma" (69)—at least for a while.

[xx] Woodmen Press, document at Beinecke Library, Yale University.

Chapter IV

Gone Fishin'

Some stories told to us in childhood anchor us. My mother told one story over and over again about their year in New Mexico. It was about a particular fishing trip. She never told stories of my father's illness. But she told this one. For me, New Mexico and fishing are always linked. They mark a place in my memory where my father's illness is interrupted. I see him as a lithe, strong young man, loving the outdoors with my mother and loving to fish, to fly fish. I see him serene by streams.

Twenty-five years after my grandparents moved from New York City to Connecticut for my grandfather's health, my father decided to go west for his, to Albuquerque, with my mother. Once again, a new place offered the hope of healing from a microbe that refused to be conquered. My father was wise to take his TB seriously. In the 1940s the cure rate was only 50%.[i] This time, however, my father opted not to go into one of the many sanatoria in New Mexico. Perhaps he had had enough of sanatorium life. Perhaps they were too expensive for him. And, he was getting married.

The Lost Time of TB: A Daughter's Story

Since the early 1800s people had gone west for the "cure." Even after Koch's discovery that a microbe caused tuberculosis, in the absence of curative medication people still hung on to the idea that the right climate and fresh air were crucial for healing. Who could blame them? The medical establishment even before WWI argued that sanatorium care rather than climate was better,[ii] yet going into a sanatorium meant giving up personal freedom. And it cost money and disturbed family life. My father was out of step with the doctors. He wanted his life, his married life. He must have felt better in Colorado. Why not try again out west, free from sanatorium life?

Why Albuquerque? Thousands of tuberculosis sufferers had migrated there between 1880 and 1930, but this migration was over by the mid 1940s. New Mexico had aggressively promoted itself nationally as the land of wellness, a disease-free paradise. The New Mexico Bureau of Immigration urged tuberculosis victims "to partake of the territory's 'pure, fresh, life-giving air.' "[iii] The state of New Mexico needed Anglos to populate it in order to gain statehood. Welcoming "lungers" was their strategy. But after "lungers," as TB sufferers were called, crowded its cities, sometimes in tents, and infected the native population, the state put the brakes on. One sufferer who had moved to Colorado years before my father headed west was forced to move from boarding house to boarding house once the proprietor discovered that this man had consumption. He said, " 'Colorado is most glad to welcome the contents of the purse the invalid brings with him, but she would prefer that the invalid not accompany the purse.'"[iv] By 1914 New Mexico's Commercial Club warned readers, "don't come to Albuquerque...if you are broke."[v] By 1945, the message was: don't come, you will infect others here.

    I imagine my father heard about Albuquerque the way utopia lives on in the public imagination, facts to the contrary. Perhaps his own father dreamed of going there. Or his doctor may have recommended he go.[vi] Perhaps he had read one of the many journals in which New Mexico advertised, or one of the recovery narratives.[vii] Somewhere he had heard the phrase, "Why Albuquerque will make you well."[viii] In choosing New Mexico as their destination, and it was likely my father and not my mother who thought of it as a path to health, he was but following on the trail of thousands.

    And so, full of hope, my father and mother went west together. Once they got to Albuquerque, they married in Los Lunas, New Mexico on March 1, 1945. They rented an apartment in a two-story building that still stands. I looked for it when I was in Albuquerque. It was still there. I took a photo and sent it to my mother, who said little. Though it was their first home, too much time, too much pain, had gone by. Flat roofed, unremarkable architecturally, the apartment suited them well. My father was asked to supervise his fellow tenants in exchange for free rent. I have no idea whether the landlord or anyone else there knew my father was a consumptive. His thin body was certainly telling. I don't know if he told anyone, even his fishing

The Lost Time of TB: A Daughter's Story

friends. He worked at a gas station to which he could walk, outdoor work. He likely got work because so many of the desperate who had come earlier and looked for work had left.[ix] My mother applied for a good clerical job in the county government and got it. She was likely the major breadwinner. Perhaps they both got jobs in 1945 because so many were still away at war.

And, they went fishing. They became close with two other couples, taking regular fishing trips with them (my father was an avid fly fisherman, as well as a bait fisherman). Once they went off on a five-day fishing trip with a guide on mules to Emerald Lake in Durango, Colorado. The elevation was high. This did not seem to bother my father. My mother wrote in her memoir, "he was gaining weight," her only allusion to his health. He did go to a lab in Albuquerque to have a chest x-ray. I am prevented from seeing these as well as all the others, so I have no way of knowing how sick he really was. But the story I gleaned from the New Mexico days was that he was indeed better there. For years my parents' New Mexico license plate hung in the rafters of our barn in Connecticut.

My mother's endlessly repeated story about fishing at Emerald Lake tugged at me as I was writing this book on tuberculosis, as did the occasional sight of a grey steel box that sat in the attic not far from the box containing the pages my mother left me. For years this box, my father's fishing tackle box, sat unopened in the attic of our family home, unopened so long that the jar of worms was utterly desiccated. Just as his TB eluded me for almost all of my life, so did his love of fishing. The attic held this other late treasure, bringing me a happier portrait of my father.

I first focused on this box one day in 1972, twenty years after my father's death. At the time I was with a man who loved to ice fish. He began talking with my mother, who mentioned one day that there was an old chest from my father in the attic. I went upstairs with him. We opened it. It was filled to the brim with tackle, both fly and bait fishing tackle. I was too afraid to look deeper into the box. I often think it was my boyfriend's interest in that tackle box that convinced my mother she had met her future son-in-law. She hadn't.

I didn't think much about the tackle for years. The boyfriend was gone, and I was not ready. But then in 2012 a college friend from Colorado invited me and her roommate out for a week, ostensibly to plan signs for our upcoming 45th reunion. (We spent about an hour at night, after cocktails, dreaming these up). One of the things we did during our week together was go fly fishing. My friend was an avid fly fisherwoman and wanted to treat us to a day on the Frying Pan River. Suited up (really I looked quite ridiculous with my high waders and a cowboy hat), guides keeping us from falling in the stream so we could stand, we all fished. As our fathers had done.

Objects release the spirit of our ancestors. But so do parallel movements of the body. There was something in the arch of my back and the stoop when bending over with the net that newly connected me with my

The Lost Time of TB: A Daughter's Story

father's body, a body which had also fished in Colorado. The fly-fishing casting body, says Conor Sullivan, is a "thing of beauty...To make a perfect cast is to feel in tune with the world."[x] This time it wasn't his sick body. It was his joyful, fishing body. I began to realize that my father must have found some respite from worry in fly fishing.

A few more years went by. Then one day in 2021, my husband and I invited to lunch a friend who was also a fly-fishing guide. After we ate, he put the fishing box my brother had brought up to our house right on the table. And then he slowly, reverently, removed each object, each fly my father had tied, each reel, all sorts of things I had no knowledge of, things used in the 1940s. A small smile lit up his face as he touched and named each one. These were not the most expensive tools. My father was fastidious, but not rich. They were honest tools. The contents of the box reminded our visitor guide of his own father's tackle box. But he also remarked on my father's care in wrapping up his reels and keeping everything in its right place. It must have taken my father a lot of time, he said, to put everything back once he took it out. I saw for the first time my father's love of his art, his patience, his care. I would come to understand a lot more about how he could survive what was to come with the elegance and understatement that he did. And I loved the guide for knowing him. I loved knowing my father in this way, at last. These were the only objects I had that were his, except for the leather folio. The metal tackle box with

Eileen Sypher

its leather handle is still in my dining room, now on the floor. I love nearly tripping over it from time to time.

I began to read more and more about fly fishing. In addition to the many books on best technique and best places are a number of meditations on it. One of the best of these is Maximilian Werner's *Black River Dreams: Meditations on Fly Fishing*.[xi] The very distance to the rivers, the need for silence, aloneness, even as one travels with a few friends, seems to invite reflection and memory. He notices all the details of the place, details that the angler must attend to in order to read the fish. The writer spends hours and hours over days wading in many streams, two or three companions not too close. They camp together, pass knowledge back and forth. The writer knows the fish so well, and other animals nearby, respects them, and winces as he remembers his early blunders that caused them harm (they were practicing catch and release). One gets a sense of these days spent on the rivers and lakes as utterly full. Some say there is no room for any other thought.

Some writers recognize the power of the respite of fishing to heal. Thomas McGuane says, "I am afraid that the best angling is always a respite from burden. Good anglers should lead useful lives, and useful lives are marked by struggle, and difficulty, and even pain."[xii] Fly fishing has even become part of the healing program for victims of PTSD.

My father would not have spoken in their words. He was not a writer. He would speak more like someone I

The Lost Time of TB: A Daughter's Story

grew up with, someone whose father owned the Esso gas station where we always got our gas (how I loved the smell). His father fished locally, with other men from Chester, including one of my father's brothers. The day I spoke with him he became wistful. He had not many words. But the memory of his father fishing was stilling, hallowed really. He himself took up fishing, passed from father to son. He said what writers have said in much more detail: one has to pay total attention, to the sky, to the minnows, to the line. Of course one is totally quiet, waiting. One is forgetting, I hope, the TB ravaging your insides.

My mother's own stories about Emerald Lake had their own spare stillness. When I look at the pictures of it now, I see none of the lake's majesty from my mother's stories. Rather I see only patient mules carrying the six up the mountain. They are all alone there. I see them setting up camp. I see the three men fishing and fishing and fishing, standing in the lake, catching the trout to eat. They wouldn't have gone too far in—in none of the photos do I see my father wearing chest waders to keep out the cold. But I know they fished all day long. And I see the women cooking all the fish in frying pans over the fire, breakfast, lunch, dinner. I have a few photos, the best one of my father proudly holding up a string of trout. In another, he and my mother are sitting on a log, he with his arm around her. My mother always ended her stories with the one about her refusing to get on her one-eyed mule to go back. She and another woman walked, in riding boots. She

Eileen Sypher

was sore for days. I saved her jodhpurs. Besides a couple of photographs of her there, that is the only object of hers I have from that trip.

What strikes me about my mother's story now is the simple stillness and simple pleasure of it. They were in a place apart, together, a place where they just fished, ate, and slept, in quiet, in peace. It was her perfect moment, a moment in which my father was doing what he loved, fishing in clear mountain air. It was a moment in which he was well, lithe, tanned, smiling, and sitting on a log with his arm around her. It was the way to remember him.

When they came down the mountain at last, they heard that the Armistice had been declared. The war he couldn't serve in was over. Four months later I would be conceived in their Albuquerque apartment, a surprise, since my mother was told she could not have children. Four months later they got in the car and drove back to Connecticut, with me in her womb, a couple of rugs from Mexico and a tray. I and the tray are all that is left. The license plate has disappeared.

For years I thought my parents left New Mexico to come back because of my impending birth. When I saw their apartment building I wept because I then knew they were coming back anyway. But they were coming back to sickness. They were coming back to death.

---

[i] "Fear, Embarrassment, and Relief," 1.

[ii] *Chasing the Cure*, 120.

The Lost Time of TB: A Daughter's Story

[iii]*On the Road*, 276.

[iv]Ibid., 282.

[v]*Chasing*, 159.

[vi]*Chasing*, x.

[vii]Rothman, 163, provides examples of some of these miraculous cure narratives.

[viii]*Chasing*, 113.

[ix]Ibid., 3.

[x]*Fishing the Wild Waters*, Pegasus (New York, 2021), 159-160.

[xi]Hancock House, 2021.

[xii]*The Longest Silence: A Life in Fishing*, Knopf (New York, 1999).

Chapter V

Speaking Pain

What in God's name do you know about pain, you who are only beginning? Do you think there. is no pain in rotting in your bed for years until one day you drown in your own blood? Do you think that there's no pain in knowing you're a pariah? Do you think there is no pain in having to apologize for your sickly presence everywhere you go, in being shunned by your friends because they think you a plague-carrier, in being afraid to kiss a girl in case she finds out that you've got TB?[i]

To be competent to speak of pain is to speak of pain that isn't yours. This requires experiencing pain that is yours. Pain experienced as if it were your own.[ii]

I have put this off long enough in this story. I am certain my father was in periodic pain before they left for New Mexico. He certainly was upon their return, as his TB intensified. They came back to the little house he had been given, a house that needed renovation. He worked on that during the day, designing the kitchen, adding two rooms, fussing that the doorknobs worked

The Lost Time of TB: A Daughter's Story

well, all while we lived with my grandparents in the next town. This is where I slept on the porch as an infant, all the time. He went fishing, occasionally, with his brother, up to Vermont. He went down to the woods to dig up the little swamp maple to shade our house. And he held me. I have the photos of him in the sunny yard holding me up in front of the birdbath, holding my hand. It was not all bad. But it was coming. I count no stories of his being ill during the three years we were together. The only stories were about foxes raiding the hen house, the mouse he caught in my bedroom, my mother asking him to use better language around me, and the like. Normal stories--except for what was happening underneath.

He had to have been in pain. I knew much about my mother's as she aged. She would talk about it with me. Until now, I never tried to imagine his. He left me no words. Nor did anyone else. And now it haunts me.

I wonder, did he talk with one of his brothers about his pain, maybe the one who was also suffering? My closest friend, who died from chronic lymphocytic leukemia in 2017, could share with me on the telephone many details of her suffering. Few were in her inner circle, her husband, her sister, me. But surely my father would spare my always worrying mother? And I doubt he would share it with his doctor. Physicians, one doctor argues, find "chronic illness messy and threatening. They have been taught to regard with suspicion patients' illness narratives and causal beliefs."[iii] And this, written in 1988. TB, in

Eileen Sypher

1943, was already an old, familiar story. No need for details. Furthermore, I doubt my father experienced "excessive rumination, magnification, and helplessness" when he was in pain. He was not a "catastrophic" type.[iv]

I now think that the silence around my father played some part in my choice of a profession. English Literature, in particular the nineteenth-century novel, focuses on a domestic world in which riveting physical pain is alive but hidden. Women with days-long migraines are upstairs in George Eliot's *Adam Bede*. Esther Summerson in Dickens' *Bleak House* heals from the worst of her smallpox in a room closed to the reader most of the time. The starving poor are visible for only a second in Jane Austen's *Emma* as a woman bringing food opens the door. In a little book she wrote called *On Being Ill*, Virginia Woolf, who herself suffered much pain, laments how little is written about pain in novels.

> *Novels, one would have thought, would have been devoted to influenza; epic poems to typhoid; odes to pneumonia, lyrics to toothache. But no; with a few exceptions...literature does its best to maintain that its concern is with the mind; that the body is a sheet of plain glass through which the soul looks straight and clear, and, save for one or two passions such as desire and greed, is null, negligible and non-existent.*

She vehemently disagrees with this lack of physical

The Lost Time of TB: A Daughter's Story

detail.

On the contrary, the very opposite is true. All day, all night the body intervenes; blunts or sharpens, colours, or discolours, turns to wax in the warmth of June, hardens to tallow in the murk of February. The creature within can only gaze through the pane.

She goes on to sympathize with the novelists:

Those great wars which it [the body] wages by itself, with the mind a slave to it, in the solitude of the bedroom against the assault of fever or the oncome of melancholia, are neglected. Nor is the reason far to seek. To look these things squarely in the face would need the courage of a lion tamer.[v]

I am in bed with influenza: what does that convey of the great experience; how the world has changed its shape; the tools of business grown remote; .... We would need a new language and different priorities: love must be deposed in favour of a temperature of 104; jealousy give place to the pangs of sciatica; sleeplessness play the part of villain, and the hero become a white liquid with a sweet taste...[vi]

But I also think that it was my career, however much I wanted to avoid exploring my father's years'-

long pain, that led me at last, slantwise, into it. The writers I subconsciously chose were guiding me. Naipaul's editor, Diana Athill, says, "Underneath, or alongside a reader's conscious response to a text, whatever is needy in him is taking in whatever the text offers to assuage that need."[vii]

So many of the writers I loved suffered from and alluded to tuberculosis. Was this an accident? Perhaps. So many of my friends and colleagues who also love these writers do not know about their TB. But it was these writers who opened a door for me.

And it was, particularly, their poetry. Woolf recommends turning to the poets.

We break off a line or two and let them open in the depths of the mind, spread their bright wings, swim like coloured fish in green waters...We grasp what is beyond their surface meanings, gather instinctively this, that, and the other...which the poet, knowing words to be meagre in comparison with ideas, has strewn about his page to evoke, when collected, a state of mind which neither words can express not the reason explain. Incomprehensibility has an enormous power over us in illness...[viii]

So, for example, Keats does not describe his brother's pain while he is dying from tuberculosis. In "Ode to a Nightingale," written as he began to feel that he too had the disease, he describes "the weariness, the fever

The Lost Time of TB: A Daughter's Story

and the fret," where "youth grows pale and spectre-thin, and dies; where but to think is to be full of sorrow and leaden-eyed despairs." I read these lines for years and never knew they were also about tuberculosis.

Or, for years I would often walk up the nearby long hill to the farm where my father grew up. I found myself quietly reciting the opening lines of Keats' "La Belle Dame Sans Merci." These lines comforted me. They somehow spoke to some inner, as yet unacknowledged condition. "O What can ail thee knight at arms, alone and palely loitering/The sedge has withered from the lake, and no birds sing." There was something in those lines. The pale knight, hollowed out. The aloneness. The withered, quiet landscape. Keats was ill when he wrote this poem. He knows he will likely go the way his brother did, young, having not, he says in his sonnet "When I Have Fears," "gleaned his teeming brain." He imagines himself in some medieval landscape, a lady without mercy holding him in thrall. Nature is dying. He is dying, but he doesn't name his disease in the poem. It is, of course, the disease that is mortality, but the image of paleness is most hauntingly tubercular. These images, repeating in me, I now think, prepared me to name and then probe my father's disease.

These words of Keats were rich in evoking, as Mallarme puts it, "little by little an object in order to show a state of soul, or inversely, to choose an object and release from it a state of soul through a series of unravelings."[ix] There was the withered sedge. The dumb birds. The pallor. All words from someone else

Eileen Sypher

that stuck, that released in me a state of soul. I didn't for a long time have any way to say more about that state.

As part of my halting movement into my father's pain I also gravitated toward reading books on other kinds of pain, for example Alphonse Daudet's (1840–97) *In the Land of Pain*. Julian Barnes, who edited and translated Daudet's notes, says that "when it became his time to suffer, Daudet discovered that pain, like passion, drives out language. Words come "'only when everything is over, when things have calmed down. They refer only to memory, and are either powerless or untruthful.' "[x] Daudet, who suffered and died from syphilis, records staccato moments: "strange aches; great flames of pain furrowing my body, cutting it to pieces, lighting it up...hypersensitivity of the skin, loss of sleep, then coughing up blood...."[xi] It is unbearable, this, for the reader as well.

Then I, again, who knows how, came upon some words from a young boy, son of a wealthy southern slaveholder in Macon, Georgia. Part of the boy's journal began in 1860 when he was twelve, published as *I Am Perhaps Dying: The Medical Backstory of Spinal Tuberculosis Hidden in the Civil War Diary of Leroy Wiley Gresham*.[xii] This material is nestled within a seven-volume journal describing life in the south at that time, material displayed at the Library of Congress Civil War Exhibit in 2012. Although Gresham's leg had been crushed in an accident, later study revealed that he suffered from pulmonary and spinal tuberculosis

The Lost Time of TB: A Daughter's Story

(the latter known as Potts disease). The editor notes that although TB has been around forever, this is a rare extended account of a patient's suffering from it.

LeRoy most frequently mentions, in his one sentence daily entries, his cough: "incessant," "troublesome," "obstreperous," "exhausting," "annoying beyond measure," "a continual hacking." His back weakens so he cannot sit up, his throat is sore, he has terrible headaches, he loses a lot of weight, and has bloody dysentery. He has an "exceedingly inflamed" abscess, "painful beyond measure." "Sick, Sick, Slept under Morphine." On June 9, 1865, he ends his diary with the words, "I am perhaps...(dying)." It is a miserable chronicle of TB days.

Soon I was prepared to begin delving into books in which physicians speak of tuberculosis. So, for example, a description of the stages of tubercular pain:

In the first stage, the patient feels a "dry, persistent cough, an irritation in the throat, pains in the chest and shoulders, a slightly accelerated pulse, and some difficulty in breathing, particularly during exercise." The second stage, which might come on suddenly, or after years, involved a "severe, frequent, and harassing cough...mucous materials and pus...hectic fever... ulcers ...in the throat." In the third, and terminal stage, "emaciation...eyes...sunken in their sockets... 'death rattle' cough...pain in the joints constant...diarrhea...legs swelled." And the death? "Anything but beautiful...excessive sweats...choking...a profuse hemorrhage, pouring from the mouth and nostrils, and causing an almost instant suffocation." Dr. William Sweetser, whose descriptions Sheila Rothman, professor of public health at Columbia, quotes, ends his list by saying, "'In the majority of instances, the mind maintains its integrity to the last.'"[xiii]

To the last, the mind registers each unbearable moment of pain. The mind knows. When someone dies suddenly, we hopefully ask, "did she feel any pain?" But what about those who die slowly, mind intact? No wonder I didn't early on look for such books. I can barely write these things now.

Or this: a description of what my father may have looked like from the *outside* as his TB advanced:

'Voice hoarse, neck slightly bent, tender and stiff; fingers slender but joints swollen; severe wasting of the fleshy parts leaving the bones prominently outlined;...The nose is sharp and slender, the cheeks are prominent and abnormally flushed; the eyes are deeply sunk in the hollows but brilliant and glittering;...the slender parts of the jaws rest on the teeth as if smiling but it is the smile of cadavers....The muscles of the limbs all wasted... The shoulder blades are the wings of the birds.'[xiv]

And this is what he might have looked like *inside*, upon autopsy, had there been one:

...small semitransparent grains, greyish or colourless, ranging in size from a millet to a hemp

The Lost Time of TB: A Daughter's Story

seed...developing the 'crude of immature' tubercles. These were either larger, individual lesions, 'yellowish and opaque...[later] with the consistency of 'very firm cheese.' [Growing into a mass, the as-yet crude tubercles] 'soften and finally liquefy.' [Two kinds emerge.] Either thick pus, a deeper yellow than before but without any smell, or a curd and whey mixture part opaque cheesy material, part thin, colorless (unless blood-stained), transparent liquid.[xv]

Nineteenth-century French physician Rene Laennec goes on to describe how these masses push aside the blood vessels and bronchial tubes, as they move into the lungs or other organs of the body. Laennec claims, as I can imagine, that these tubercles were associated with great pain, coating the intestines, collapsing the spines in some cases, invading the lungs so breathing was difficult.[xvi]

I doubt any doctor then or now would tell his or her patient in such agonizing terms what was happening inside the sick body. Perhaps to protect the patient, or to protect the doctor's imagination, the words are not these but more generalized ones. Nor do x-rays, even if my father saw his in any detail, communicate such things as smell, color and strategies of invasion.[xvii] There is a cultural wall around this kind of communication. Today the closest we get to imagining this kind of thing is seeing a graphic autopsy suite on a television program. And, even then, the body is in stasis, the rivulets of pain stopped for the viewer.

What, then, did my father *feel*, for we know that people experience pain differently? Where is this recorded? I have no letters. No diary. No words from my mother. No words from his siblings. Had my father been an educated man in the 19th century perhaps he would have left me a diary or letters, describing his illness while also sparing me. Perhaps his siblings, too, had they been educated in this pain discourse, would have spoken with me, offering at least comfort and advice. But I doubt it. Just as obituaries never talk about pain, neither do the people we love. It is unseemly.

Such visceral descriptions of pain are rare (neither Daudet or Gresham intended their words to be published). By the middle of the twentieth century pain language would become more forthright. Even had he been an educated man, my father in the 1940s likely would not have left many words at all.

Some of his silence, however, was the product of his medical treatment. By this point in the history of tuberculosis in particular, the patient was no longer a "subject" navigating his or her own pathway through a mysterious illness, observing the signs, making decisions about where to travel for health, etc. Rather, by the twentieth century the tuberculosis patient had become the "object" of a medical discourse increasingly opaque to most patients.[xviii] The doctors spoke, the patients listened.

This discourse included a novel form of quarantine,

The Lost Time of TB: A Daughter's Story

the sanatorium, which, separating patients from family and familiar locations, attempted to mold patients to be compliant and silent in the name of healing. Most of them were. The door that shut me out from him also silenced him.

---

[i] The Rack, 35–6.

[ii] Sharon Cameron, *Beautiful Work: A Meditation on Pain*, Duke Univ. Press (Durham, 2000), 1.

[iii] Arthur Kleinman, M.D., *The Illness Narratives: Suffering, Healing & the Human Condition*, Basic Books (New York, 1988), 17.

[iv] Lalkhen, Dr. Abdul Chaaliq, *An Anatomy of Pain: How the Body and the Mind Experience and Endure Physical Suffering*, Simon and Schuster (New York, xxxx), 17.

[v] Woolf, 32–33.

[vi] Ibid., 44.

[vii] Tompkins, 3–4.

[viii] Ibid.

[ix] *Atlantic*, 2/17/19. Add Civil War Boy diary

[x] Knopf (New York, 2002), v.

[xi] Ibid., 6–7.

[xii] Dennis A. Rasbach, M.D., Savis Beatie (California, 2019).

[xiii] Rothman, 16–7.

[xiv] Areteus, quoted in Davey 3.

Eileen Sypher

[xv] Rene Laennec, *Spitting Blood*, 60.

[xvi] Ibid.

[xvii] Foucault, in *Birth of the Clinic*, speaks of the dominance of the ocular, the gaze, in the language of pain. The x-ray undoubtedly was born out of or contributed to this.

[xviii] Ibid.

Chapter VI

The Red Brick Sanatorium 1951-2

Sanitorium, a healthy place. Sanatorium, a healing place.[i]

The locus of servitude and freedom, mortal illness and the possibility of rebirth, a breach in the ordinary course of a human life, a place in the world (and its own world) but not of it, a waystation en route to an uncertain destination...the sanatorium is the lungers' purgatory, a 'vacant space' preserving no 'trace' of those who have passed through.[ii]

However much the sanatorium resembled other institutions, it had one unique feature—the omnipresence of the shadow of death.[iii]

At last I am at the place I had forgotten about for so long. From now on, the story isn't good at all. The locked door of the sanatorium now rises up before me. Perhaps a locked door was kind to me at age five, though it felt violent. I could no longer see him smiling down at me. The windows in red brick were too small and too high up. I could no longer see where he slept. I could no longer hear him. No photographs. No tele-

Eileen Sypher

phones. No letters even. Now Undercliff is all rubble. I can no longer physically retrace his footsteps. Instead, I have to stitch together others' photographs and accounts of such places, 471 of them in the United States by 1935.[iv] Now all the sanatoria are gone or repurposed. Few remember them.

In the fall of 1950, my brother but ten months old, my father left us. I don't even remember the day. He had to go into the hospital in New Haven, Connecticut, where he stayed for eleven weeks. It must have been sudden, perhaps a major hemorrhage, for he left that jar of live worms in his tackle box. He had never been overnight in a hospital before. I do not know how they treated him there. I have a photograph of me, in a knitted winter cap my mother made for me, crouched on the outside steps. I am looking away from the camera, curled up, holding onto an entrance pillar, as if I knew he was going away from me. As if I knew the pillar was all I had left. I am glad that they, my mother and aunt, brought me with them that day. After eleven weeks, he entered a tuberculosis sanatorium, Undercliff Sanatorium in Meriden, Connecticut.

xxx

Here's what I can learn about his new home from local papers and from the books about the sanatorium movement. The descriptions are unemotional. They serve me as a safe entry point.

Connecticut's sanatoria took their place within a

The Lost Time of TB: A Daughter's Story

vast national network of public and private institutions. Sanatoria seemed to crop up quickly on the country's horizons in the first half of the twentieth century. By the middle of the 1800s tuberculosis sufferers began to go to fresh-air respites and high altitudes, thought to be a help in the cure. But by the early 20th century the full-fledged sanatorium movement was launched. Once Koch's discovery in 1882 that TB was contagious and not hereditary gained traction, the public was scared. TB was everywhere, unseen, silent for a long time, but, once activated, usually lethal—and contagious. In the absence of antibiotics, unavailable until the 1940s, campaigns to improve life in crowded slums and farmhouses, breeding grounds for contagion, and campaigns to sequester the ill became vigorous. There was, in this period of "optimism in social engineering," as Caldwell says, "an unprecedented degree of regulation."[v] Some of the sanatoria in the nation were financed partly through F.D.R.'s Federal Public Works Administration. Some were devoted to special classes of TB patients, such as Civil War Veterans, African American patients, and mental patients.[vi]

An entirely new kind of institution devoted to quarantine, the sanatorium was born to combat TB. Once x-rays, sputum examination and tuberculin skin tests were able to identify people with active TB, TB's victims were urged to leave life as they knew it. They were asked to commit themselves to months, even years, of living an entirely new life apart from the places and

Eileen Sypher

people they had known and loved, a life in which they were expected to be submissive. If the desire to get well was insufficient to motivate them, the fear of reprisal against their families worked. Erving Goffman has called such places "total institutions," life carried on in the same place, under one authority, in the company of others similarly afflicted; time, food and activity were strictly regulated.[vii] This was the quarantine place of the first half of the twentieth century. After the sanatoria closed in the 1970s, surveillance continued through community centers, developed in response to some of criticisms of cloistered sanatorium life.[viii]

In 1901, the State of Connecticut gave Hartford Hospital $25,000 to create a special tuberculosis hospital. Wildwood Sanatorium opened in 1902, housing fifty patients, many of whom were in advanced stages. The cost to the patient was $7 a week (my maternal grandfather was then making .09 cents an hour at a local piano factory). In 1904 a second sanatorium was built in Wallingford, Gaylord, for patients in the earlier stages of the disease. By 1909, a year after my paternal grandfather moved his family to Connecticut, the State increased its funding for Wildwood and Gaylord, began to try to control tuberculosis in cattle, and authorized the creation of several state-operated facilities.[ix] Annually, TB was killing 252 of every 100,000 people living in the state. It was then the leading killer in Connecticut.[x] By 1934, TB killed fewer than 50 out of 100,000. The containment campaigns seemed to be working. Sanatoria were a big part of this.

The Lost Time of TB: A Daughter's Story

Undercliff was one of four public sanatoria built in Connecticut about 1915, the others being Uncas on Thames in Norwich, Laurel Heights in Shelton, and Cedarcrest in Hartford (1939). These were public institutions, but one still had to pay. Despite a claim in *The Hartford Courant* in 1982 that care was free,[xi] there was in fact a sliding scale, depending on one's ability to pay.[xii] Only in neighboring New York was the cost free. In Connecticut, numerous local TB associations took up the cause of raising funds, partly through the sale of Christmas seals, and educating TB nurses. I don't know how much my father had to pay or if he ever knew the amount. It would have troubled him. In his and my mother's hometown, some of the very people who were on the Christmas Seal committee were members of their church.

Thoracic surgeries were first performed only at Uncas, then later, by 1949, at Cedarcrest as well. Initially Undercliff housed tubercular children, the first in the country,[xiii] but in 1933, after much local struggle, Seaside Sanatorium for children was built in Niantic so that they could take advantage of a new therapy, heliotherapy.[xiv] As children began to leave Undercliff, Undercliff in 1939 became a haven for adult tubercular patients, many of whom had been factory workers in Meriden. In 1954 it closed as a tuberculosis sanatorium. becoming a hospital for the elderly, and then, in 1956, came under the jurisdiction of the Department of Mental Health. When it was decommissioned in 1976, other state facilities occupied the

Eileen Sypher

grounds, until the buildings were eventually demolished. I cannot go to the grounds even now. Police actively patrol the area.

Undercliff, and indeed all of Connecticut's sanatoria, were very well respected by the public and the press. An article in 1940 describes them this way:

> The sanatoria were a pleasure to visit, modern, well-equipped and staffed by enthusiastic, intensely interested physicians. There are 32 full-time physicians, 5 part-time dentists and a consulting staff of 15 physicians. This gives a better ratio than the 1 doctor to 50 patients set-up as stated in the Pennsylvania Plan of Tuberculosis Eradication.[xv]

The article also praises Connecticut for having no waiting list, unlike other states (although an article from 1942 claims there were waiting lists.)[xvi]

These are the bare bones of the history of this place to which my father was headed. But that is all they are, bare bones.

xxx

I don't know how my father made the trip, or if my mother was with him. Undercliff, forty acres nestled under Meriden's Hanging Hills, was reached by a long winding road in. I linger on a video made by a maintenance worker at another Connecticut sanatorium that

The Lost Time of TB: A Daughter's Story

had, by the time of the video, become a mental hospital. The video was taken on the last day before the facility closed. The man holds the camera through the windshield, as he slowly follows another twisted road in. Not a soul is in sight. I imagine getting into the car with my father. I try to get inside his head and his heart as he follows the winding road into Undercliff.

Mercifully my father would have had some inkling of what lay ahead. He might remember from his days at Woodmen's what it was like to be looked upon as a patient, an invalid. But then, he had fewer responsibilities. Now he would be suspending not only his life as brother, friend, and fiancé. Now he was also husband, father, breadwinner. He might be looking forward to rest, time to heal, time not to worry about hurting his family further by giving them his disease. His wife's parents were taking care of the children, while his wife went back to work. I like to think he imagined he would walk out a well man. Still, he must have felt shame that he couldn't provide for his family any longer.[xvii]

Before he left he might have talked with other people in the town who had been to one of the sanatoria in Connecticut, in our area likely Uncas on Thames or Undercliff. Perhaps the neighbor who became his roommate was already there. But he may not have even told others where he was going or why. This was quite typical of people as they headed off.[xviii]

My father and my mother also might have read, before he left, Betty MacDonald's *The Plague and I*.

Eileen Sypher

MacDonald, a popular writer with a sense of humor, had earlier written a best-selling book called *The Egg and I*, about her life as a poultry farmer, which my parents then were. After her stay in the Firland Sanatorium in Washington State, MacDonald wrote *The Plague and I*, published in 1948. It is one of the rare longer first-person accounts of life inside. It was condensed in a magazine my mother regularly read, *Good Housekeeping*. She comments on being sent to an institution: " 'be it penal, mental, or tubercular, is no game of Parcheesi and not knowing when or if you'll get out doesn't make it any easier. At least the criminal knows what his sentence is.' "[xix] While her book shows the woman patient sticking it out for the good of her health, *The Plague and I* was not, despite its often cavalier attitude, a particularly rosy picture of life inside.

As my father prepared to go to the sanatorium, he never likely knew the statistics of sanatorium survival, for which I am grateful. Doctors rarely shared such information with their patients. Between 1900 and 1940, after which streptomycin was used to begin the cure in earnest, 25% of TB patients died in the hospital. 50% of those released from sanatoria succumbed within five years of discharge.[xx] Historian Frank Snowden says, "there is no robust evidence that the therapeutics devised during the decades of the war on tuberculosis were more effective than traditional humoral approaches" (323). Perhaps, he goes on to say, the optimism about sanatoria helped lift the patients' spirits. And perhaps that was all.

The Lost Time of TB: A Daughter's Story

In the night perhaps my father worried that he would never again look upon some of the faces or the woods that he loved. That he would soon fade into oblivion. That he would soon be buried in a new grave where my mother and her parents would later be buried. That his only son would not remember him. That his only daughter would bury him deep inside, sometimes not even thinking he was real. I hope not.

I wonder as he drove into Undercliff if he also thought about his decision to go. He did not have to go, by law that is. He got into that car by choice. Here is a medical and cultural peculiarity: few states had laws that forced people with TB to go into sanatoria, thereby removing them from the public.[xxi] How was it that there was such seeming laxity around quarantining those with TB? It was contagious. For a time there had been a war on it. Yet states shied away. Perhaps this laxity stemmed from the disease's elusive, slowly appearing nature. As well, it attacked rich and poor alike. In the cities immigrants and the poor whose " 'dissipated and vicious habits' endangered the health of the community" were sometimes forcibly confined; they were made to work rather than rest.[xxii] My father was a country man, not rich, but not poor either. No one demanded that he go. And he could rest.[xxiii]

There was also no law that said patients had to stay once they arrived. As late as 1957 an article in *The Hartford Courant* urged the state to build a security treatment building in which to forcibly house TB patients who "have no sense of responsibility" and so leave the sanatorium when they wish. Speaking in favor of the bill were a doctor from Yale and the President of the Connecticut Tuberculosis Association.[xxiv] The bill failed, as did one to prevent alcohol in the sanatoria.

I think his going was not an easy decision. He would so miss watching his young children grow. He would so miss leaving his wife of but five years. But my father was mature and in pain. His wife and daughter already carried the latent germ. He had, I think he felt, no choice.

xxx

As my father approached Undercliff, he would notice that it looked nothing like the last sanatorium he was in, Woodmen's in Colorado. There were the hills of Meriden (it was named for being under a cliff), but not the glorious mountains of Colorado. And instead of Woodmen's charming private cottages, which followed the plan of the nation's first sanatorium in Saranac, N.Y., he saw a large, forbidding brick building with several wings. A huge staircase led to the entry doors. Off to one side were the nurses' quarters. This was not the kind of place, like Woodmen's, that would invite someone to take a photo of my father, in his suit, standing next to a nurse outside one of the cottages. I have only seen the aerial drawings and the photographs taken of the outside, without people. I cannot remember what I saw at five.

The Lost Time of TB: A Daughter's Story

To my eye, the photographs of these places are all dismal. I prefer the old wooden structures of Undercliff, with their wrap-around porches. But these were replaced by brick buildings. Though designed by architects, to my eye they have little grace. Eugene O'Neil felt the same way when his father, en route to New York City, dropped him off at the Shelton Sanatorium. O'Neil was mortified to be going to a state institution. When he got off the train from New London in New Haven, three coffins in a baggage truck rolled across his path. He left for Gaylord, where his doctor told him "he'd meet a better class of people."[xxv] Gaylord, also, looked better.

It is hard to tell from the aerial photographs of Undercliff if any attention was paid to the patients' desires to go outside or to the views they would see from the rooms. This was not true of some other sanatoria. Before the medical establishment fully embraced the idea that TB had a bacteriological source, numerous sanatoria grounds featured lawns, fountains, pleasing paths--all to entice people out of doors. Landscape architects like Frederick Law Olmsted designed some of these. Later, landscape played less of a role as pharmacology took over. Landscape was expensive to maintain. It wasn't any longer needed. Undercliff's grounds were nothing like those of Saranac Lake in the Adirondacks: pleasing lakeside views, privacy. Nor were they like those of the award-winning Paimo in Finland, a renowned example of modernist architecture designed by Alvar Aalto and now a visitors' site. Paimo featured vast grounds and open-air pavilions, serpentine paths marked with fountains and flower beds. It is still beautiful.

If the hospital was off limits to me, a small child, the sanatorium was in another world. The imposing, cold buildings, typically set apart in fields to sequester patients from the general public,[xxvi] haunted the lives of family on the outside, changing them perhaps as much as it did the lives of those inside. For those of us who grew in rural places, these buildings were a visual shock. Family on the outside did not know much about what went on in there nor did most of them dare ask. They could not visit for long. Children were not allowed. No wonder when I talk to my neighbors now about those days, while not one family seemed to escape the scourge of tuberculosis, no one can say much about sanatorium life. Even now, years later, people remember the sanatorium's name, but that seems to be it. Not only were there few words about a patient's pain, there were few words about life inside. One day I asked my cousin's wife, whose father was at Uncas-on-Thames Sanatorium in Norwich, Conn, what his life there was like. She had no words for that. All she could say about her father was that when he was released he slept on a separate bed in her parents' bedroom and moaned all night. When I tried to ask her another question, she turned away.

Though in other places around the country sanatoria have been repurposed, this was not so in Connecticut. Here they are all shuttered, some demol-

The Lost Time of TB: A Daughter's Story

ished. Connecticut's sanatoria became emblems of another, often scary, time. Weeds choke Seaside, as it waits to become a state park. Undercliff is now utterly gone, demolished. All that is left visually of it now for me is, at best, on postcards. At worst, there are photos and videos of it after it was abandoned. After the last of the mental patients left, the windows were broken, the weeds grew, papers cluttered the floor, paint chipped, toilets stopped up. I traveled on You-tube with a few young men as they broke in and made movies with their cell phones. They had no idea what they were looking at. They could not imagine people, real people, living their lives there, people like my father. I try to drown out the primitive sound track by remembering a Chopin Ballad in my head, Chopin, himself a sufferer, whose haunting melodies in the minor key speak to me of tuberculosis, interludes of darkness followed by shorter moments of light. The buildings are gone. I cannot go in and remake a movie. I wish I had never gone back.

---

[i] Caldwell, 70.

[ii] Gilman, 15.

[iii] Rothman, 238.

[iv] Caldwell, 91.

[v] Caldwell, 183, 180.

[vi] *Hartford Hospital 125th Bulletin*, Vol. 32, No. 2, May 1979.

Eileen Sypher

[vii]*Asylum*, 1961, 6. Critics have said sanatoria varied in their degree of discipline and totalizing effect. See Staffan Bengtsson and Pia H. Bulow's "The Myth of the Total Institution, Written narratives of patients' views of sanatorium care," www.elsevier.com/locate/socscimed (Social Science and Medicine), 2016. They argue that patient letters from Sweden reveal acquiescence was not total.

[viii]Mason, et al, 212, 214.

[ix]"The Healing Triangle: Hartford Hospital's First 150 Years," In-house publication.

[x]Harrison and Jones, 2015.

[xi]"Whatever Happened to Tuberculosis?," 7 February 1982.

[xii]"State Urged to bear cost of TB Care: Legislative Council May Advocate Ending 'Financial Means Test,'" *Harford Courant*, 4 May 1952.

[xiii]Meriden Record and Journal, Saturday June 14, 1956.

[xiv]During the early 1900s children were particularly afflicted by bone and glandular tuberculosis (undoubtedly from drinking raw milk from infected cows). Heliotherapy, exposure to sun and wind, was thought in Europe to alleviate symptoms and so Connecticut began to plan for Seaside Sanatorium in Niantic for children. There were two earlier sites considered, one in Westbrook, one in Clinton, with each saying no to the state, out of fear of contagion. They did not realize that the type of TB to be cured there was not contagious, as pulmonary TB is. The first Seaside was built after much struggle in the legislature. Insufficiently financed initially, at last the commissioner found an abandoned hotel in Niantic, buying it through a third party to avoid the kind of confrontation they had experienced in Westbrook and Clinton. Neighbors initially complained bitterly, but once their petition was overturned, by one vote, they later apparently acquiesced. Commission narratives claim that Connecticut was the first state to aggressively pursue sunbaths as a therapeutic technique. This was largely due to the influence of Dr. Stephen Maher who had gone to Europe and studied the success of French sanatoria which used heliotropy, sun and wind and water. Mayer did much to turn public opinion around, allaying neighbors' fears.

Given the number of ill children, a second Seaside was built in Waterford, opening in 1933. It is the most architecturally interesting of the sanatoria.

The Lost Time of TB: A Daughter's Story

It was designed in the Tudor Revival Style by renowned architect Cass Gilbert (who also designed the Supreme Court Building in 1935). This style was more residential than institutional in its appearance. In its first two years, only five of the fifty nine patients died. By 1939 the death rate in Connecticut from TB was 32.4 per 100,000.

[xv] Editorial Comment, *Diseases of the Chest*, Official Organ of the American College of Chest Physicians, Vol. VI, October 1940, no. 10.

[xvi] "State Faces Increase in Tuberculosis," Hartford Courant, 10 April 1942.

[xvii] While men felt shame over not being the breadwinner, women felt shame over not being able to care for their children and worried about whether they would be forgotten. See "Tuberculosis Sanatorium Regimen in the 1940s: A Patient's Personal Diary," Journal of the Royal Society of Medicine, 2004, July, 350-353.

[xviii] Caldwell, 212.

[xix] Rothman, 229.

[xx] Caldwell, 116.

[xxi] See Mooney on Britain, 154. There were not enough sanatoria in the early decades, so the emphasis was on promoting hygiene in domestic settings.

[xxii] Rothman, 209.

[xxiii] Laxity about quarantine of course is present in our own time. In the history of contagious illness much needs to be done to account for the enforcement of rules. Undoubtedly whether or not infractions are punished has to do with class and race. As late as 1984 a prostitute named Carlotta Locklear was outed as a carrier of AIDS by *The New Haven Register*. She was subsequently arrested, ostensibly on another charge, and shortly after died in the hospital. Scott W. Stern, "An AIDS Activist's Archive," New York Review of Books, October 29, 2021.

[xxiv] April 12, 1957.

[xxv] Arthur and Barbara Gelb, O'Neill: Life with Monte Cristo, New York (Applause, 2000), 371 & 374–5.

Eileen Sypher

[xxvi]American sanatoria, originally in urban centers, moved increasingly to the country, where it was felt good air and freedom from temptation, seen then as a contributing factor to acquiring TB, would help the sufferer. The moral argument for the character-building dimension of rural life was used by early campaigners. But the isolation of these early sites did not always sit well with patients. In an account from 1948, a patient writes about arriving at one of these early institutions. "We entered the Pines by a long, popular-lined drive...magnificent gardens. It might have been any small endowed college except that there were no laughing groups strolling under the trees." She thought she might as well have bought a one-way ticket. Institutions built after 1910 tended to be nearer cities and showed the same healing rates.

Chapter VII

Going In

One afternoon I visited a woman in town, a family friend, once my grandfather's nurse. Someone told me she had contracted TB when she was a young nurse and had to stay in a sanatorium for a few months. Over tea, I asked her to tell me what it was like. Smiling, she said that she found her stay pleasant. She liked her single room. She made life-long friends. She had a radio. And, she said, the very ill were sequestered down the hall. She couldn't hear their coughs. She is a strong and optimistic woman. Yet, she said to me at the end, a truth emerging, "I stood at the window one day, looking down at the cars going by. And I wept."[i]

I have so very little to go on about what it might have been like for him. Pat Nelson was able to read the records of patients that were left behind after the sanatorium in which her parents worked in Minnesota had closed.[ii] Lynn Downey contacted the site manager where Arequipa Sanatorium in California had been located. "History can pivot on the actions of just one person," she says. The manager had decided to keep all the old papers in the sanatorium when it closed, so saving a forty-six year archive of letters, photos, patient

Eileen Sypher

records, scrapbooks.[iii] Living in Connecticut, I was not so lucky. My father's records, and those of others who had been in the sanatoria, are locked up in the State of Connecticut Archives, never to be seen by anyone. Nor did my mother save any letters my father may have written to her while he was inside.[iv] I am staring at a blank page. I have to imagine.

And so, undoubtedly winded, he climbs the long stairs into Undercliff that day in 1951 and walks inside. I have no photograph of him standing outside the building, as I do of him at Woodmen. My mother didn't want to take that picture.

Someone would welcome him. Was he or she pleasant, engaging my father? Or was it a rote speech? It would go something like, "Leave the old life behind." And, "here are the house rules, written up in a little book for you." Perhaps Undercliff's was just like the "Welcome book" given out at the nearby sanatorium in Shelton. There will be no smoking (my father was a smoker then). There will be no drinking. These are the hours for complete bed rest. These hours are for meals. Use a sputum cup when you cough. Cover and try to control your cough. Though the sanatorium movement was to change in the first half of the twentieth century (the idea of the power of wild places to heal subsiding), Caldwell observes that the devotion to the patients following a rigid schedule did not.[v]

The message of the Welcome Book was two-edged: follow our rules, and this place is "all for you." You need "cheerfulness" to get well. You also need to be

The Lost Time of TB: A Daughter's Story

"courageous."[vi] The underlying message was: "mystery and complexity" will be banished from your life, because we are in charge.[vii] You will have no private life here.

Would he be stunned? Or did he remember the rules at Woodmen's, the rules of factory life, the rules his father laid down? But this had to be different, this time. The stakes were higher. And he was sicker. This was the last hope, the last stop, before healing, or dying.

I see him entering his room, my mother beside him, for a while. He had a roommate, someone he knew from Chester; his wife and my mother became friends. But I have no photographs of this room, or even inside Undercliff as it was during my father's year. There was no patient who took photographs as there was in Minnesota,[viii] at least none that have been found. And my mother never told me anything about it. I guess she never wanted to go back inside herself.

I doubt his room had been designed like Paimo's award winning rooms. Aalto, having been a patient himself, developed a more humanist approach to modernist functionalism than other sanatoria architects at the time.[ix] Aalto is now recognized as a pioneer in the "evidence-based design movement," officially defined in 2003 (and still in its infancy in 2009) as a movement to base design on achieving the best possible outcomes, in the case of patient healing. In his later writings on Paimio, Aalto considered the issue of patients' psychology in relationship to architecture. He felt that attending to patients confined because of TB he could learn a lot about the effects of space on people. He studied patient living quarters so he could design to protect them from the pressures of a collective environment. For a bed-confined patient, in a long and painful situation, he believed the room could not be an ordinary room, but rather one filled with soft colors that changed. Ceilings should be darker, artificial light not coming from above but from in back of the head, heat should be directed at the feet and not the head, the beds should be placed to provide natural light, and at least one wall should be sound-proofed. Every room was to have a sink for each person (some rooms were two person rooms, some four). He also discouraged the use of tubular and chromium furniture, not good for human touch. Furniture needed to be washable, but patient-friendly. And so he developed flexible wooden furniture. His reclining chair, the Paimo Chair, best for a patient who found it difficult to breathe, is still in use today.

No, my father's room was nothing like this. I suspect it was clinical, grey, dimly lit. Perhaps the windows were dirty. Maybe there was only one window. Nothing was to be put on the walls—not antiseptic enough. Maybe he had a radio. Maybe my mother often brought him a few flowers. Maybe he had photographs of us. I wonder which one he had of me. My mother years later assembled a few infant photos of me in a frame—perhaps it was one of those. I look at it every night before I go to sleep, to remember myself

The Lost Time of TB: A Daughter's Story

then, as I was in his eyes.

I try to imagine the nature of his days. It was not like that in the most famous novel about a TB sanatorium, Thomas Mann's *Magic Mountain*. There, as Rothman so aptly describes it, "pampered patients" lie swaddled in blankets outdoors, eat "hearty meals," and engage in "lengthy discussions." They go to lectures, take walks. Doctors and nurses urge patients to take their temperatures and go for x-rays, but it seems often left up to one's neighbors to remind one of meal times. So seductive it all was that Mann himself had to get away from it all when his wife was a patient there.[x]

Nor was Undercliff like Saranac, America's first sanatorium, modeled by Trudeau after European ones, in its remote comfort. Though patients were gradually acclimated to spend time outdoors and fed rich food,[xi] Caldwell, who provides the best description of it, calls Saranac "a more rustic and democratic place, nearer to a summer (and winter) revival camp than a haunt of the rich."[xii] I still come across people whose relatives were "somewhere in New York."

My father, on the other hand, was fortunate not to be in a sanatorium like Riverside in New York. There indigent and uncooperative patients were confined, against their will. Hospital or prison, Rothman questions? Otisville in the Catskills, funded by Hermann Biggs, New York's health officer, as was Riverside, argued that the poor should be cured by work, no "coddling."[xiii]

My father, instead, was in a "state" institution, at a

time when being outdoors and eating rich food were seen as irrelevant to cure. I see him rather like the equivalent of a worker on the assembly line, working to put himself back together in the presence of ugly machinery. Gone were the wrap-around porches at Undercliff's clapboard buildings. In their place were red brick walls with small windows.

The daily routine at Undercliff had to feel punishing to my father. No getting up in the sun-filled front room with my mother, me in a room next door. No walking out to the farm kitchen for coffee. No walking down the gravel driveway into the red barn to check on the chickens, five hundred of them, listening to their morning sounds, looking for the newly laid eggs warm under the pullets. No smelling the fresh air as he came out, seeing the expanse of sky, loving the so-well known trees around the barn and house, the little swamp maple he had just planted. And seeing that field behind: red foxes in the morning, deer. And all those unexplored woods in the back, hundreds of acres of them, places where he sat, found arrowheads, tried to pet chipmunks. This is the place where my house now sits.

No, here, he had to stay put, others ordering his days, new, antiseptic smells, new sounds of wheels in the hallway, coughs, few familiar faces. He had to stay put, largely in bed.

Sometimes I imagine I can hear the voices of the doctors as they made their rounds. I am not sure they would be honest—honesty between doctor and patient came later. I don't think they suggested any non-sur-

The Lost Time of TB: A Daughter's Story

gical procedures. At the time my father entered the hospital and later the sanatorium in Meriden, painful procedures such as artificial pneumothorax, in which a lung was collapsed to allow it to rest, and thoracoplasty, in which ribs were removed, had been largely dropped in favor of drug therapy. Painful procedures, still used in Europe at this time, structure A.E. Ellis' novel *The Rack*—as in rack of torture. But for my father there would likely be no painful insertion of hypodermic needles and lancets into the bones of his ribs, splintering them, to draw out his marrow blood for analysis.[xiv] Still, what did they tell him? Did they say he was in bad shape? Did they offer any hope?

I don't know what kind of pain medication he would have been given. I don't know if he even spoke of his pain to anyone. One he surely would have been given was streptomycin, an antibiotic drug only available after 1946 and then only for those in sanatoria. If the doctors anticipated that my father would be having a lung resection, a long course of therapy with streptomycin was the protocol in the United States at this time.[xv] Used singly, however, streptomycin did little. Some TB bacteria became resistant to it. George Orwell was given streptomycin for his TB, but he suffered an allergic reaction to it. Orwell did leave his sanatorium, restored somewhat after rest and being outdoors, but he was never well after. He says, "'To walk even a few hundred yards promptly upsets me...I cannot so much as pull up a weed in the garden...I can't type much because it tires me too much to sit up at a table.' "[xvi]

Eileen Sypher

Orwell went again to a sanatorium, this time a private one. A new drug was tried, unsuccessfully, because his lungs were too far gone for further intervention. Perhaps Orwell was given isoniazid, at first used in combination with streptomycin. But at this point nothing stopped Orwell's hemorrhaging.

My father might have been given isoniazid. It was not until 1952, however, when he was very ill and preparing for surgery, that a combination of drugs, isoniazid, rifampicin, and pyrazinamide, began to be used to arrest TB. This combination was highly effective. My father, however, was too far gone.

Despite, or because of, its regulated ways, there was patient discord within sanatoria, patient resistance, however subtle. Even in the idealized Paimio, there was discord. Patients recalled they did some garden work if they were able or sewed in special rooms. They also cleaned their own rooms and made their own beds. They had some time for reading and ample time for visiting others. The rules, however, were very strict. Time for visiting, for reading, for working was regulated. And so normal life was lost to the necessities of a large institution. Patients responded by developing "play" periods, with patients having different names for different units and games organized accordingly, some allowing time for courting couples. But sometimes they reported disturbances, particularly in large wards with young people. Young patients became restive at the number of hours they were to stay in bed. And the staff's character had a huge impact on the patients, some staff

The Lost Time of TB: A Daughter's Story

hyper-vigilant, some preferring to ignore what went on. Staff reported that while alcohol and smoking were forbidden, these caused most of the problems. Patients felt they did not have enough entertainment. Those writing on European institutions concluded that while many entered the sanatorium full of hope and happy about ample food, after a time, and after painful procedures, the young, especially, at times became despondent. TB began to be described by the 1950s as as much a psychological disease as a physical one. Rules were relaxed as the typical time at a sanatorium lessened.

Patients could leave if they chose, and between 10 and 30 percent did, though many returned.[xvii] But once one committed to staying, rules and regulations, an entirely new culture, fortified the wall between the inside and the outside. Days of lying in bed, being subjected to strict routine, stripped of familiar occupation, urged to say nothing to others of bad things, of fears, even of others' deaths,[xviii] one's letters from the outside in some cases censored so as not to disturb,[xix] one's books carefully selected in the library[xx]: all created that wall.

A 1947 article about veterans who left the sanatorium against medical advice (AMA) reveals much about why some tried to leave. Within one year over half of the patients at veterans' sanatoria were "irregularly discharged," which means they walked out. The article goes on to detail a study of what caused people to walk out—was it VA sanatoria in particular? All sanatoria?

Eileen Sypher

Or, was it just personal reasons? The study discovered that irregular discharge at a wide variety of public institutions was very high, ranging from 32-83% of patients. Professional social workers were called in to interview those who had gone AMA. What they discovered was that while familial problems were usually involved in a patient's decision, as well as a patient's immaturity, much of the problem rested with the institutions themselves. Patients complained that they had not enough time with their doctors, so they didn't understand what was happening to them. They felt that the nurses sometimes seemed uncaring.[xxi] They had problems with how the institution was set up, the strict rules, the layout of the wards, the failure sometimes to separate severe from less severe cases, the difficulty in getting passes to move about or go home for a visit, boredom, etc. The study recommended increasing staff and attending to patients' emotional needs as well as their needs for information. The article stresses that the TB sanatorium is not like other institutions: one is there for a long time, one carries the stigma of having TB, and one is confined to bed often in the prime of life.[xxii]

But some did thrive in the silent sequestered space of the sanatorium. Eugene O'Neill writes of his sojourn in Gaylord: "my mind got the chance to establish itself, to digest and value the impressions of many past years....At Gaylord I really thought about my life for the first time...undoubtedly the inactivity forced upon me by the life forced one to mental activity..."[xxiii] But Gaylord was a privileged place. And O'Neill was well,

The Lost Time of TB: A Daughter's Story

not too sick and already a writer.

The sanatorium was a culture that promoted acceptance and silence. How patients could be brought to accept that having TB would institutionalize them, the first disease to occasion this, is a nut that is hard to crack. Foucault guides us in the arc of this change in *The Birth of the Clinic*. He argues that toward the end of the eighteenth century the human subject is gradually redefined. Once under the gaze of the clinical physician, the patient is turned from a subjective human, with a rich personal history, into an object for scientific universal study. The growth of the sanatorium, from places of respite for the wealthy into places for the ordinary, may be seen as the apex of the clinical movement, a visible place in which the gaze of both physician and onlooker was magnified. In fact, in later photos of Undercliff, when it was a mental hospital, there was an observation kiosk in the middle of the patient floor. I don't know if it was there in my father's time. I, too, as a child, gazed up at his window from the lawn. In his remote confined apartness, he was marked as sick, while the rest were healthy. When he looked out, on the other hand, he knew he was left out. One patient, Harriet Lowenhjelm, speaking of her prolonged stay in a sanatorium, says, "I feel left out—or rather left in. Landscapes used to be for walking. Now they are merely for watching. The sense of belonging has disappeared."[xxiv]

But conforming to this gaze, to this reduction in one's personal life? How does the patient conform? I can only guess. Other doors must have seemed closed to my father. He must have been convinced there was no other way for him to try to get well. Once inside, would he not be changed? What would it be like for him not to roam in the woods, look into the eyes of his wife and children, his dog? There was little time for talk of this with others, busy nurses, other patients also trying to suppress their private histories in order to survive. Perhaps this all happened so gradually that he barely noticed. He would, like the others who stayed, become more and more compliant with the rigid rules of sanatorium life. Not a rebellious man, not one who criticized the government, he was material for a perfect patient. The rural culture he grew in valued independence but he was not paranoid about hospitals. Nor was he afflicted with one of the diseases, alcoholism and the like, that led many to run away. None of the rest of us got to see how he was changed. What would he have been like coming home? I remember visiting, with my mother, my father's roommate after my father died. I remember him lying in bed, saying little, vacant in a way. He died several years later when the family moved to Arizona.

We have few stories of the process of such acquiescence. Arthur Frank in "The Wounded Storyteller" says that "Telling stories of illness is the attempt...to give voice to an experience that medicine cannot describe."[xxv] There are lots of snippets from patients, snippets which Rothman says reveal "unrelenting hostility."[xxvi] Yet there are few first-person memoirs and

The Lost Time of TB: A Daughter's Story

novels exploring sanatorium life, full-blown pathographies, written before 1950, by which point tuberculosis was on the decline and sanatoria were closing.[xxvii] These longer accounts largely feature acquiescent patients. Mann's *The Magic Mountain* reveals patients accustomed, even attracted, to a long life inside. Less well-known and far grittier than Mann's novel, Ellis's (a pseudonym for Derek Lindsay) *The Rack*, responding to Mann's portrayal, chronicles the life of a poor student in a hill sanatorium in France who is subjected to terrible food and various painful procedures—procedures largely hidden in Mann's novel. Ellis' doctor says to the patient, Paul, "Consider yourself an experiment of the gods in what a man can endure" (315). Yet even Ellis' characters seem to accept being there.[xxviii] Blai Bonet's *The Sea* (1958) is a memoir of his time in a sanatorium in Spain following the Civil War. Though it is not structured around the gritty details, it sees the sanatorium as a place whose proximity to death can bring about a moral reckoning.

There is really only one pre-1950 American full-blown pathography, Betty MacDonald's *The Plague and I*, set in her time in the Firland sanatorium in Washington state.[xxix] Hers, the only one to focus on female patients, though replete with "jarring notes,"[xxx] features largely subdued patients. Though they complain—the need for better food, hot water bottles, etc.—they comply.[xxxi] Her comedic style subdues the criticism.

Undercliff has its own partial pathographies, snippets written by patients for its in-house journal, *Cliff Hangers*. I doubt my father contributed, but he likely read it. I understand the desire of writers such as Gilman to make a lot of these in-house publications. So many on the outside, like me, hunger for details. His study says patients and staff "contributed poems, essays, letters, anecdotes, gossip, reminiscences, book reviews, comic pieces and jokes, plays, notices of current events, and medical advice."[xxxii] Gilman says that although there were rich and poor sanatoria, patients' experiences were remarkably similar. Among these, he argues, was an emphasis on reading and writing. The newsletters regularly solicited contributions from the patients as a form of therapy: literature could alleviate pessimism and anxiety, which were hurtful to health. Few budding writers, however, notes Gilman, flourished in the sanatorium. Caldwell has a somewhat different take from Gilman on these publications. He argues that there were generic boundaries, that people were expected to be optimistic in "folkloric" rather than "literary" ways.[xxxiii] Flights from reality were therapeutic in ways that ironic detachment was not.[xxxiv]

Evidence on patient attitudes of acceptance is provided by a couple of studies of other partial pathographies—in diaries, letters, journals. In her account of New Mexico sanatoria, Nancy Owen Lewis says that those who recovered seemed to maintain a connection with the place and the doctors as well as with other patients. She cites former patients signing a letter in tribute to a physician and one patient who came back

The Lost Time of TB: A Daughter's Story

to visit. This man saw his fellow patients as "one big family."[xxxv] On the other hand, in 1980 a group of former patients and staff in Sweden collected memories of patients between 1910 and 1957. Patients reported that the prevailing order inside was not easily challenged. They felt clearly separate from the staff, some of whom they labelled "bad."[xxxvi]

There are, however, rare voices of outright complaint in these partial pathographies. In a 1947 letter to the editor of *The American Journal of Nursing*, a woman patient takes issue with an earlier description of life in one sanatorium as "heavenly." Her husband was at war. She had lost her baby. Her life was falling apart. But when she would ask to talk with a nurse about her condition, out of her terrible worry, she was told, " 'Oh, for heaven's sake. What are you complaining about? There are plenty worse off than you."[xxxvii] Such comments are reminiscent of MacDonald's portraits of nurses from the late 1930s in *The Plague and I*. The patient says she has a "horror" of ever going back there again. The memories arouse "bitterness" and "panic."[xxxviii]

On the other hand, perhaps things were better by the time my father arrived. An article in the same journal from 1951, written in two parts, one by a nurse, one by a former patient, describes their experiences at Undercliff. The article is uniformly positive. The nurse says that for about a year they have wanted to take "dry routine" out of nursing and develop closer bonds between patient and nurse. They wish to see the

89

Eileen Sypher

patient as more of an "individual" with a whole life. To this end, first the nurse studies an entry profile. When the patient arrives, the patient-education supervisor spends time with him and his family going over the routine, then introduces him to the other patients on his ward. The nurse claims that this helps the patient feel that he is not a stranger. Other nurses, during that first week, teach him techniques for minimizing contagion. She claims that teaching replaces the former "police-like policy" of earlier days. The patient's days are filled with radio talks and lectures on the illness, thus encouraging a sense of self-control and eliminating mis-information passed along by roommates. Visits by adult family members are encouraged. Perhaps letter writing is too—and perhaps the letters aren't censored. Prior to discharge, the patient, the staff hopes, is well-prepared. The result, she says, is a better image of the institution in the community.

The patient in the article, well-spoken, and well-educated, echoes the nurse's testimony. He says he begins to feel emotionally as well as physically supported. He adds that he is also spiritually cared for, telling us about the church services. He thanks the Undercliff personnel for their expert care as he goes off to teach at the University of Bridgeport.[xxxix]

It is clear from this article that public perception of the sanatoria by 1951 was not uniformly positive and so changes had to be made. I like to think my father benefited from this kind of atmosphere.

The Lost Time of TB: A Daughter's Story

***

I saw him at home only twice during his year at the sanatorium. On one spring day he walked me down the hill to the vernal pool at the bottom of our sandbank that borders the woods. The tadpoles were swimming, so it was maybe the spring before the surgery that killed him. So I was four or five at the time. I don't remember those tadpoles, but I do remember the walk back up the hill. He, so tall, in his long dark coat, was holding my hand. I looked down and saw a tiny pink salamander in the grass at my feet. I looked far up into my father's eyes. I said, "Daddy, will this grow up to be a dinosaur?" He smiled at me. He didn't laugh. He didn't say much. But what he said was calming. He said, "No, it won't." And all my fear of a monstrous world went away, at least for a while. And maybe his did, too. Maybe he held on to this memory of us while he was lying in bed.

For he would remember me when he went back. I know this. But I was never sure that he did, for I never heard from him. He was a fleeting presence, here for a moment, then gone, somewhere into the ether.

---

[i] Interview with Ruth Thayer, Fall 2019.

[ii] Nelson, Open Window: *The Lake Julia TB Sanatorium A Community Created by Tuberculosis*, 2020.

[iii] Lynn Downey, *Arequipa Sanatorium: Life in California's Lung Resort for Women*, University of Oklahoma Press, 2019.

Eileen Sypher

[iv] May Krugerud met an eighty-year old woman who had saved the letters she wrote as a thirteen year old patient in another Minnesota sanatorium. Krugerud edited these in *The Girl in Building C: The True Story of a Teenage Tuberculosis Patient*, Minnesota Historical Society Press, 2018.

[v] Caldwell, 71. In Saranac, the order was: 7am, awake, 8 breakfast, 8:30 out of doors, 10:30 lunch when ordered, 11:00–1:00 exercise or rest, 1:00–2:00 dinner, 2:00–4:00 rest in reclining chairs, reading, but no talking, take temperature, 3:30 lunch when ordered, 4:00–6:00 exercise in prescribed amount, 6 supper, 7 out on good nights, 8 take temperature, 9 lunch and bed. 79.

[vi] "Welcome Book," Conn. State Library.

[vii] Caldwell, 93.

[viii] Nelson was directed to Art Holmstrom, former patient at Lake Julia. Art saved many photographs he had taken while he was inside during the 1940s.

[ix] What TB did for Modernism, 6. See Diana Anderson, "Humanizing the hospital: Design lessons from a Finish sanatorium," *Canadian Medical Association Journal*, 2010 August.

[x] Rothman, 226.

[xi] Ibid., 203.

[xii] Caldwell, 45.

[xiii] Rothman, 209.

[xiv] *The Rack*, 84.

[xv] Livingstone, 248.

[xvi] Mason, et. al. argues that "strong echoes" of the sanatorium are found in *Nineteen Eighty Four*, 212.

[xvii] Rothman, 245.

[xviii] Richard Sucre ("The Great White Plague: The Culture of Death and the Tuberculosis Sanatorium") says that in both the Piedmont and Blue Ridge

The Lost Time of TB: A Daughter's Story

Sanatoria in Virginia, there were no services for the dead. The staff was "required to remain apathetic to the death of a patient." (p. 5)
[xix]Snowden, 311.

[xx]See Jennifer J. Connor, "Prescribed Readings: Patients' Libraries in North American Tuberculosis Institutions," *Libraries and Culture*, Summer, Vol. 27, no. 3, 252-278. She says one library at a VA hospital wanted *The Magic Mountain* removed, because it drew attention to the self, rather than to courageous people.

[xxi]An early report on Connecticut's first tuberculosis Sanatorium, Wildwood, annexed to Hartford Hospital (1902–1939), contains the following description of the patients. The "patients themselves are very hard to please, owing to the nature of their disease, and great difficulty has been encountered in retaining competent employees....The handling of the patients has been equally trying...The patients go to the Sanatorium too ill to work, and not ill enough to be confined in bed; and naturally after a certain length of time life becomes monotonous, and the period of contentment wears off, then many of them become restless, discontented, and fault-finding. However, everything possible has been done to keep them happy and contented." "The Healing Triangle: Hartford Hospital's First 150 Years."

[xxii]An article discussed in Part II, on nursing at Undercliff in the 1950s, is about redressing some of these general problems in sanatoria.

[xxiii]Caldwell, 227–8.

[xxiv]Jonathan Wistrand, "Sanatorium Narratives from the Baltic Sea Region and Early Signs of the Pathological Genre: The Case of Harriet Lowenhjelm," *Explorations in Baltic Medical History* 1850–2015, Ed. Nils Hansson and Jonathan Wistrand, Univ. of Rochester Press (Rochester, 2019), 196.

[xxv]Dietrich, "Patients and Biopower," 3.

[xxvi]Rothman, 228. See 231-234 for examples of patient adverse reactions to the rule books.

[xvii]One particularly interesting piece of American writing, less open to representing TB than European writing, is Eugene O'Neil's 1921 play, "The Straw," which recounts his short stay at Gaylord Tuberculosis Sanatorium in Connecticut, founded by David Lyman, one of the national founders of the anti-tb movement. It was a private institution with a long waiting list. The daily drama is the weigh-in. People who lost weight lived in fear that they

would be shipped off to state institutions. A young girl is at the center of this play, her fiancé nervous about getting near her once he learns of her diagnosis. The play shows how the father of the young victim is pressured to let her go by the threat of members of the local TB Association, generally wealthier people, stepping in. O'Neil apparently loved his stay. "...my mind got the chance to establish itself, to digest and value the impressions of many past years....At Gaylord I really thought about my life for the first time...undoubtedly the inactivity forced upon me by the life forced me to mental activity..." (Caldwell, 227–8) O'Neil's reaction to the sanatorium is not as high-flown as Mann's, whose central character, Hans Castorp, finds the sanatorium, "a shrine of initiatory rites, a place of adventurous investigation into the mystery of life." (Mann, "The Making of the Magic Mountain," 719–29 in Lowe-Porter's translation of *The Magic Mountain*.)

[xviii]Caldwell says that the European narratives, full of "grim realism," were very unlike the American ones, which were "tales of optimism." 109.

[xxix]*The Girl in Building C.*

[xxx]Caldwell, 115.

[xxxi]One that I have not been able to read is discussed in Caldwell. Isabel Smith, a patient at Saranac Lake, wrote "Wish I Might" about her three- year stay. Caldwell observes that she responds to the life as she is supposed to: docilely. Her attitude is one of optimism, "the vapors and the blues are allowed in, but only to be mocked away" (104–5). She keeps a "Trouble Book" for no one else to see (107).

[xxxii]"The Poetics of Lunger Lit" from *Yiddish Poetry and the Tuberculosis Sanatorium: 1900-1970*. Ed. Ernest B. Gilman, Syracuse Univ Press, 2015.

[xxxiii]Ibid., 105.

[xxxiv]Caldwell, 124–5.

[xxxv]227. Caldwell notes that in 1955 Firland, where Betty MacDonald was a patient, conducted similar interviews with similar results among the patients. Some of these responses he attributes to the difficulty so many patients had leaving the sanatorium environment. 124-5

[xxxvi]*Myth of the Total Institution.*

[xxxvii]"Letters," "Tuberculosis Hospitals and Sanatoria," *The American*

The Lost Time of TB: A Daughter's Story

Journal of Nursing, vol. 47, no 1, Jan 1947, p. 48.

[xxxviii] Ibid.

[xix] Vol 51, no 10, Oct '51, 592–593.

Chapter VIII

Surgery

The captain of all these men of death that came against him to take him away, was the Consumption, for it was that that brought him down to the grave.
  —Bunyan, *The Life and Death of Mr. Badman*

My father left Undercliff Sanatorium in early June of 1952 to go to Hartford Hospital to have what is called a "lobectomy," in his case the removal of two of the three lobes of his hopelessly diseased right lung. He was told that, if he wanted a life with his children, this was his only option. It was an operation of "'heroic'" proportions.[i]

In the 1940s the practice of performing lobectomies had been abandoned because of the high rate of post-surgical complications. But by the 1950s the attitude changed. In an article published in 1950, two years before my father's death, the argument is made for more extensive surgery to remove part or all of a lung, since most cases of TB show infection to be most intense in one lobe.[ii] The procedure started in 1906, but attempts were largely unsuccessful. Now the

The Lost Time of TB: A Daughter's Story

authors argued, with improvements in surgical and anesthetic techniques and the use of streptomycin, there were fewer chances for post-surgical complications.[iii] The authors, however, say that long-term results were not yet available. My father was one of the pioneers in the new push for lung removal in the 1950s.

My father would have been prepared for his lobectomy and possible lung resection surgery by having undergone bed rest. He was also likely given streptomycin (ironically discovered through a chicken farmer) during his time at Undercliff. The other drug that my father may have been given, since it, like streptomycin, was also introduced in 1944, was para-aminosalicylic acid, or PAS. Administered in liquid form or in cachets of paper taken with water, it was foul tasing and difficult to swallow. In 1951 another drug, isoniazid, was discovered that, combined with the others, lessened the proliferation of resistant organisms.

My father went to the Cedarcrest Building at Hartford Hospital, where all TB patients were sequestered who were preparing for lung resection surgery. Two hundred and fifty lung procedures were performed at Cedarcrest in 1949, using its own surgical residents when it opened (because of a huge state-wide backlog); thereafter for some years some one hundred lung resections per year were done with physician rotation from the main hospital.[iv]

My father's lobectomy surgery was performed at Cedarcrest on June 9, 1952. On June 28, my mother, at 2:15 pm, walked into his room carrying a bunch of sweet peas. She found him dead in bed. My mother collapsed in the hall after calling for a nurse. The doctor who came by wanted to know who would pay for this.

The word my mother used in her story written years later to describe what happened to my father was "succumbed." She was still protecting me. A few days after his death, sweet peas and baby's breath, given by his children, 5 ½ and 2, would be laid on his grave. My mother would never grow sweet peas again. Nor would I.

Was my mother shocked? I don't know. My aunt whispered to me once many years later that when she and her husband visited my father they found him in "not very good shape" after his surgery. Family and friends surrounding Joachim in *The Magic Mountain* know that he is about to die. I suspect my mother, somewhere, knew.

My father died from a pulmonary embolism, the most severe reaction a patient can have to lung resection. Sudden back pain, dyspnea, and shock result. A year after he died a new procedure for early detection of such embolisms would be developed: the echocardiogram. My father, again, was born too early.[V]

One of the greatest blessings of modern medicine is anesthesia. The patient under the knife doesn't know what is happening. I wanted to find out what exactly happened. A friend's father, precise yet compassionate, was a TB surgeon in the 1950s. After he stopped

The Lost Time of TB: A Daughter's Story

removing lungs and performing lung collapses (pneumothorax), he turned to cancer surgery in the 1960s.

One day my friend, then a young man, was invited by his father to witness lung removal surgery. He described to me the incision, not knowing the effect his vivid description could have on me even now. First his father cut an arc from the back side of the arm around underneath the sternum area, rather like a sickle shape, I imagine. Then the skin was lifted up, ribs removed (flung on the floor sometimes he said), while the lung removal began.

There was a lot of blood.[vi] The nurses used gauze pads to mop it up. The pads soaked in blood were thrown on the floor. Later, each one was tacked up onto a big board so each could be counted, lest one be left inside the patient.

My friend still has his father's surgical kit. While I was sitting in my friend's serene study in the middle of New England woods one recent summer's day, he lovingly and carefully opened the worn brown leather box with its elaborate hinges.

There inside I saw it all. A collection of surgical knives, hemostats, tweezers, even silk suture thread wrapped in an aged piece of toilet paper. But on one side, there it was: a small saw. A saw. For the ribs I imagine. I almost fainted. To a surgeon such tools would not be shocking. To me, student of the humanities, they seemed gruesome. To me, daughter of a man whose lung had been removed by the likes of them and who died afterward, they seemed like instruments of torture.

Bickford, et. al describe the optimal surgical position: lying prone or laterally, head tilted, so that the germs do not spread. After surgery, the authors say that the healing is generally smooth, and that the patient exudes a sense of "well-being."[vii] Breathing exercises are recommended. Fourteen days after surgery, if there are no complications, the patient is allowed out of bed. (My father only lived twelve). These surgeons in the article performed 250 surgeries. Only 2.5% of their patients died. A follow-up six months later revealed the disease was arrested in 90% of the cases.

Nurses would, of course, tell otherwise. Healing was not always smooth. As soon as possible patients were to sit up and expectorate, not with a small cough but a full-chested effort, painful for the patient. And the wounds were long and deep. I wonder how my father tried to heal. I wonder what he told the nurses about his life, his hopes, us, me. I try to imagine my father's last, likely painful, hours alone. An unnamed friend visited earlier that day, leaving a note because my father was asleep. Perhaps a nurse was there for a while, and maybe he talked. I have to brush aside accounts of patients who can't breathe as they near death. I cannot think about what he felt at the last.

I try to imagine what he looked like near and in death. I sat by my grandfather a few hours before he died and held his hand. I saw my grandmother in her last week after a long illness, spending hours in her

The Lost Time of TB: A Daughter's Story

room with her. I saw my mother's lifeless body the morning after she died, I hope peacefully, in her sleep. We had spent a wonderful day together, looking at first daffodils and first robins. I have nothing to go on where my father is concerned. My mother never told me what he looked like. All these images float in ether. I cannot touch his hands, or his face, or say words to him or sooth his awful scar. Ether. The only story she could tell was of collapsing in the hall outside his room after she found him dead in bed and the doctor. I don't even remember her face on June 28, 1952 when she walked in the kitchen door.

I imagine someone afterward sent her what are called his "effects." Among those may have been the black leather folio with his name embossed on the outside, the one in which he kept his stationery to write her letters, the one I have preserved, the one I have given to my brother--to help him remember. So little I have. Ether.

---

[i]Kirby, 613.

[ii]Livingston, James L. M.D. "Observations on the Treatment of Pulmonary Tuberculosis at the Present Time." Mitchell Lecture, Royal College of Physicians, June 18, 1954.

[iii]Bickford, B.J., et. al., "Lung Resection for Pulmonary Tuberculosis," *Thorax.* 1951 Mar 6 (1): 27.

[iv]Hartford Hospital material.

[v]On March 3 1952 *Time Magazine* reported on the cure for TB: "those who had been bed-ridden for years were now 'dancing on the wards'" (Rothman,

249). My father just missed this, too.

[vi] One British nurse viewing this procedure reported that "'blood was flowing down into the surgeon's boots.'" Interview with Nurse L, 3 March 2006, Kirby, 613.

[vii] Bickford, 31.

Chapter IX

The Long After

*I am not resigned to the shutting away of
loving hearts in the hard ground.*
—Edna St. Vincent Millay

*In certain favourable moods, memories—what one has
forgotten—come to the top. Now if this is so, is it not
possible—I often wonder—that things we have felt with
great intensity have an existence independent of our
minds; are in fact still in existence? And if so, will it
not be possible, in time, that some device will be invented by which we can tap them? I see it—the past—as
an avenue lying behind; a long ribbon of scenes, emotions. There at the end of the avenue still, are the garden and the nursery.*[i]
—Virginia Woolf

Could it be that that birdbath, my father kneeling and holding me up in front of it in 1947, does still exist? I have here tried to resurrect this moment through my words. At moments it seems as if they are enough to bring it back and me there again with him. But I know there is something else that helps. I left my childhood home, and that birdbath, when I was eighteen. But I returned to it when I was fifty. I returned to build a house, with my husband, next door to it and to my brother who still lives in our childhood home. Somehow being in place seemed necessary: to be in the very place where he and that birdbath had been. It is no accident that this house sits on the hill through which he roamed when all was woods. One of the downed logs, now nearly rotten, might be the very log he sat on, once, when he tried to pet the chipmunk. I have come to understand why so many people want to stay put, stay where their families have been. Place is powerful—and words fix and immortalize them.

Place makes memory come alive again, but it also continues to yield things, forgotten objects that speak. One recent afternoon I found some that were mine in that attic that held my mother's fragments of memoir and my father's fishing box. I sat in the corner sifting through all the school papers of mine that my mother had saved in a large file box. Sympathy notes from classmates when I had my tonsils out, high school, college, graduate school papers and course notes, my sophomoric Valedictorian speech. Way in the back were several folded-up drawings on heavy beige paper. They were dated January 1953. I was in the first grade. My father had been dead for about six months. It was six months after he died that I first spoke of him to my mother when I said, "take me to daddy's grave."

The Lost Time of TB: A Daughter's Story

It was shocking to open these crayon drawings because I never remember drawing in school. I remember saying to the art teacher in sixth grade, "I can't draw." It must be that I didn't want to draw, not after these.

The same house is in the center of all the crayon drawings. It is two stories tall, with attic windows and a steep roof. The windows are small. It is a made-up house, a displaced house from my birth house, which is one story with a gently sloping roof. I wonder if it was some version of that red-brick sanatorium into whose high windows I could not see?

In one drawing, three figures are walking away from the house. The one in front is a little boy pushing a cart. In the middle a woman is following him. Behind her is a little girl, smaller than the little boy. All are leaving the house. The boy commands the mother's attention, as my brother did, because he was younger, and I was "stronger" by my mother's reckoning. I am following behind them, too little to do much about anything. We are, perhaps, leaving that past behind. In another, the house is in a valley, the hill sharply cutting into it. A little girl flanks each side. Is she standing guard? In another, a short driveway leads from the road to the house. On the left side stands a tall woman garbed in black from head to toe. Her heart is criss-crossed with small black lines. In the last, to the left of the house stands a tree. A little girl is sitting under it, looking at the house. Between her and the house are vertical orange lines. On top of the roof of the house

Eileen Sypher

are more of the same orange lines. The little girl, I think, is watching the house burn. Or she herself has torched it.

Riveting, discovering these drawings of mine at 6. How knowing they all were. Ravaged in their crayon starkness, they cut to the quick of me even now, at 76. In a way these drawings reassure me now. I had accepted at the age of six that there was no man in the home picture. I had accepted that my younger brother needed more of my mother's attention. I expressed my anger in burning. And, in the one where I was alone with the house, I accepted that I would be standing on my own.

So, these drawings. But I am haunted now too by emerging memories of images that came to me when I was about seven or eight. I would get on my bicycle, leaving my mother weeding her flower bed. The images would come as I pedaled up the hill. I can't even remember their detail now because they horrified me. I would go back to my mother and tell her about them. Calmly she would say, "just put them out of your mind." She was not angry or surprised. Perhaps she had them too sometimes. I see now this was my rage beginning to be buried.

And then there were the dreams that I now can let loose. I dreamed once that he was still living in our town, with another wife and another daughter. I felt the bottom fall out of me. I now recognize the familiarity of such dreams to fatherless daughters.

I am just beginning to understand the drawings and

The Lost Time of TB: A Daughter's Story

these strange events. I am also just beginning to understand some of my life choices better. I have come to see that, like many fatherless girls, I early on chose men who would replicate, in my case, my father's abruptly leaving. My mission was to change the story. I failed. I failed, until I picked someone who would not go. I always considered that choice a miracle.

Who knows what will yet be birthed. But I do know that I now begin to see that parallel universe Woolf speaks of. The birdbath is as it was. He is as he was. I have here brought him back to life. I have let myself see these things, these places, these scenes, as still existing in another time frame, yes, but one as foundational as the ordinary, to me.

***

These changes, these discoveries, these surfacing memories are all part of my evolving "long after" in coming to know my father was not just a dream of mine. But a particular effect of my writing and research is my becoming achingly aware of all those now in the world, and even in the United States still, suffering from tuberculosis. Devious, tuberculosis has resisted medical attempts to stop it. It is continually evolving. Asked recently on Colin McEnroe's show on PBS in Connecticut, Heran Darwin, Professor of Microbiology at NYU, said she hoped researchers could figure out TB before she died.[ii] She went on to say that every year 1 ½-2 million people die of it, while 1/3 of all people in

Eileen Sypher

the world carry latent forms of the disease,[iii] forms that both the HIV virus and immunosuppressant drugs can activate. It is hard knowing I will likely not live to see the end of this disease.

But what I can do, have tried to do here, is encourage others to tell their stories. Few of TB's victim tell or have their stories told in any detail. Nor is the absence of story confined to those who suffer from tuberculosis. There is something about contagious diseases, perhaps the randomness of their attack, that discourages the stories that celebrate a life. As I watched the Queen's funeral, I realized how little we mourn together the loss of any person, but especially one whose illness we want to hide. My mother saved all the materials from her mother's and father's funerals in our attic. There was nothing about my father's funeral, no papers, no stories. I have no idea who came, who didn't. I wasn't invited.

Here I have tried to tell his story. I have gone to the grave and brought him back.

---

[i] Woolf, 67.

[ii] Aired Wednesday, August 31, 2022.

[iii] The CDC says ¼ of all people.

Selected Sources

Adams, Annmarie, et.al. "Collapse and Expand: Architecture and Tuberculosis Therapy in Montreal, 1909, 1933, 1954." *Technology and Culture* (2008): 908–946.

Bates, Barbara. *Bargaining for Life: A Social History of Tuberculosis*, 1876–1938. University of Pennsylvania Press, 1992.

Blum, Deborah. "The 19th-Century Fight Against Bacteria-Ridden Milk Preserved With Embalming Fluid." *Smithsonian* (October 5, 2018).

Bryder, Linda. "Papworth Village Settlement—a Unique Experiment in the Treatment and Care of the Tuberculous?" *Medical History*, (1984), 28:372–390

Caldwell, Mark. *The Last Crusade: The War on Consumption 1862–1954*. Macmillan, 1988.

Connecticut Board of Health Bulletin 1914–15. Connecticut State Library Archives.

Dairy and Pure Food Laws of Connecticut, 1923, 1919, 1915, 1913, 1911. Connecticut State Library Archives.

Diedrich, Lisa. "Patients and Biopower: Disciplined Bodies, Regularized Populations and Subjugated Knowledges," in *Treatments: Language, Politics, and the Culture of Illness*, University of Minnesota Press,

2007.

Dubos, Rene and Jean, *The White Plague*. Rutgers. 1952.

Fairchild, Amy L, et. al, "Opening Battles: Tuberculosis and Foundations of Surveillance," *Searching Eyes: Privacy, The State, and Disease Surveillance in America*, University of California Press, 2007.

Gilman, Ernest B. "The Poetics of Lunger Lit," *Yiddish Poetry and the Tuberculosis Sanatorium*. Syracuse, 2015.

Goffman, Erving. *Asylums*. Anchor Books, 1961.

Goffman, Erving. *Stigma*. Prentice-Hall, 1964.

Guest, Simon. "Cure, Superstition, Infection and Reaction: Tuberculosis in Ireland, 1932-1957," *Oral History*, Vol 32, No. 2, Memory and Society (Autumn, 2004): 63–72.

Heikkonen, Nina, ed., "Paimio Sanatorium Conservation Management Plan 2016." Alvar Aalto Foundation.

Hunsaker-Hawkins, Anne. *Reconstructing Illness, Studies in Pathography*. Purdue University Press, 1999.

Hickok, Florence H. and Francis Dolan, "Some Satisfactions of Tuberculosis Nursing," *The American Journal of Nursing*, Vol 51, No. 10 (Oct. 1951): 592–593.

Kelly, Susan. "Stigma and Silence: Oral Histories of Tuberculosis." *Oral History.* Vol. 39, #1 Discrimination (Spring 2011): 65–76.

Kirby, Stephanie, "Sputum and the Scent of Wallflowers: Nursing in Tuberculosis Sanatoria 1920-1970," *Social History of Medicine,* Vol 23, no. 3, 602–620.

Lalkhen, Dr. Abdul Ghaaliq, *An Anatomy of Pain: How the Body and the Mind Experience and Endure Physical Suffering,* Simon and Schuster e-book.

Livingstone, James L. "Observations on the Treatment of Pulmonary Tuberculosis at the Present Time," *British Medical Journal,* London (January 29, 1955).

Mason, Paul H., et. al, "Social, Historical, and Cultural Dimensions of Tuberculosis," *Journal of Bioscience,* 48: 206–232.

Mooney, Graham. "The material consumptive: domesticating the tuberculosis patient in Edwardian England." *Journal of Historical Geography,* 42 (2013): 152–166.

"A Neighbor's Story of the Modern Woodmen of America Sanatorium," Modern Woodmen Press, 1934, Beinecke, Yale University Library.

Olmstead, Alan and Paul W. Rhode, "Not on My Farm! Resistance to Bovine Tuberculosis Eradication in the United States," *Journal of Economic History,* vol. 67, No.

3 (Sept. 2007): 768–809.

Reynolds, Kristen. "Well-Built in Albuquerque: The Architecture of the Health-seeker Era, 1900–1940." Thesis. Master of Arts, History. Univ of New Mexico (Dec. 2010).

Rothman, Sheila M. *Living in the Shadow of Death: Tuberculosis and the Social Experience of Illness in American History.* Basic Books, 1994.

Snowden, Frank M. "Tuberculosis in the Unromantic Era of Contagion." *Epidemics and Society.* Yale, 2019.

Spellen, Suzanne, "Brownstoner Walkabout: The Great Milk Wars, Parts 1&2" (Nov. 8, 2011).

Sucre, Richard. "The Great White Plague: The Culture of Death and the Tuberculosis Sanatorium." Papers of Blue Ridge Sanatorium.

"Tuberculosis Hospitals and Sanatoria," *The American Journal of Nursing,* Vol. 47, No. 1 (Jan. 1947): 48.
Tufts Magazine (Spring 2019): 42–49.